The Mason Jar
COOKBOOK

80 HEALTHY AND PORTABLE MEALS

AMY FAZIO

Skyhorse Publishing

Skyhorse Publishing books may be purchased in bulk at special discounts for sales promotion, corporate gifts, fund-raising, or educational purposes. Special editions can also be created to specifications. For details, contact the Special Sales Department, Skyhorse Publishing, 307 West 36th Street, 11th Floor, New York, NY 10018 or info@skyhorsepublishing.com.

Skyhorse® and Skyhorse Publishing® are registered trademarks of Skyhorse Publishing, Inc.®, a Delaware corporation.

Visit our website at www.skyhorsepublishing.com.

10 9 8 7 6 5 4 3 2

Library of Congress Cataloging-in-Publication Data
Names: Fazio, Amy, author.
Title: The Mason jar cookbook : 80 healthy and portable meals / Amy Fazio.
Description: New York : Skyhorse Publishing, [2016] | Includes index.
Identifiers: LCCN 2016012711| ISBN 9781510704251 (hardcover : alk. paper) |
    ISBN 9781510704268 (Ebook)
Subjects: LCSH: Salads. | Canning and preserving. | Storage jars. | LCGFT:
    Cookbooks.
Classification: LCC TX807 .F37 2016 | DDC 641.83--dc23 LC record available at https://lccn.
loc.gov/2016012711

Cover design by Jane Sheppard
Cover photos by Amy Fazio
Author photos by Beck Diefenbach

Print ISBN: 978-1-5107-0425-1
Ebook ISBN: 978-1-5107-0426-8

Printed in China

To Mama, for cleaning up the kitchen, and Dad, for saying everything I make is delicious.

TABLE OF CONTENTS

MASON JAR LADY IX

A BRIEF HISTORY OF THE MASON JAR XI

MASON JAR SALAD BASICS XII

Ingredients xii

Types of Jars xiv

Putting It Together xv

USEFUL TOOLS AND MASON JAR ATTACHMENTS XVI

TIPS AND TRICKS XVII

HOW-TO RECIPES XIX

Roasted Veggies xix

Candied Nuts xxi

SALADS 1

Taco Salad 3

Red, White, and Blueberry Balsamic Caprese 5

Strawberry, Avocado, and Kale Salad 7

Guacamole Salad 9

Arugula, Pear, and Gorgonzola Salad 11

Peach Caprese 13

Cranberry and Brussels Sprouts Salad 15

Chickpea, Avocado, and Kale Salad 17

Watermelon, Feta, and Arugula Salad 19

Roasted Fall Salad 21

BBQ Chicken Salad 23

Asian Pear and Cashew Salad 25

Mango, Strawberry, and Arugula Salad 27

My Big Fat Greek Salad 29

Pear, Pomegranate, and Spinach Salad 31

Mexican Avocado Caesar Salad 33

Peach, Blueberry, and Feta Salad 35

Chinese Chicken Salad 37

Curry Butternut Squash Salad 39

Prosciutto, Melon, and Arugula Salad 41

5 B Salad 43

Chipotle Sweet Potato, Black Bean, and Kale Salad 45

Honeycrisp and Spinach Salad 47

Steak House Salad 49

Antipasto Salad with Mixed Greens 51

Rainbow Salad 53

Mediterranean Artichoke and Spinach Salad 55

Tropical Chicken Salad 57

Strawberry, Goat Cheese, and Spinach Salad 59

Broccoli, Almond, and Cherry Salad 61

Zucchini Noodle Salad 63

Orzo, Spinach, and Sun-Dried Tomato Salad 65

Mexican Corn Salad 67

Sweet Potato and Chickpea Salad 69

Zucchini, Corn, and Quinoa Salad 71

Avocado and White Bean Salad 73

Honey and Peach Panzanella 75

Buffalo Chicken and Quinoa Salad 77

Bacon and Pea Pasta Salad 79

Thai Peanut Pasta Salad 81

Fruit Salad 83

OVERNIGHT REFRIGERATOR OATS — 85

Basic Refrigerator Oats 86

Piña Colada Refrigerator Oats 86

Key Lime Pie Refrigerator Oats 86

Triple Berry Refrigerator Oats 86

Strawberry, Chocolate, and Hazelnut Refrigerator Oats 86

Apple Cinnamon Refrigerator Oats 86

Pumpkin Pie Refrigerator Oats 86

YOGURT PARFAITS — 89

Basic Yogurt Parfait 90

Piña Colada Yogurt Parfait 90

Banana Cream Pie Yogurt Parfait 90

Peanut Butter Banana Yogurt Parfait 90

Raspberry Lemonade Yogurt Parfait 90

MAKE-AHEAD SMOOTHIES — 93

Basic Smoothie 94

Berry Me Smoothie 94

Green Machine Smoothie 94

Too Good to Be Green Smoothie 94

Take Me Somewhere Tropical Smoothie 94

MAKE-AHEAD OATMEAL — 97

Basic Oatmeal 98

Chocolate Banana Oatmeal 98

Strawberry Banana Oatmeal 98

Apple Cinnamon Oatmeal 98

Cherry Almond Oatmeal 98

Pineapple Coconut Oatmeal 98

MEALS IN A JAR — 101

Breakfast Burrito in a Jar 103

Microwave Quiche in a Jar 105

Chicken Parmesan "Sandwich" 107

Waldorf Chicken Salad "Sandwich" 109

Picnic in a Jar 111

BBQ in a Jar 113

Taco Bar Picnic 115

Deconstructed Sushi 117

Instant Noodles in a Jar 119

Creamy Polenta 121

DESSERTS — 123

Banana Split Trifle 125

Sweet Strawberry Peach Panzanella 127

No-Bake Key Lime Cheesecake 129

Blackberry Crisp 131

Salted Caramel Apple Pie Trifle 133

"BRING THE BUBBLES" COCKTAILS — 135

White Wine Camper Sangria 137

Red Wine Camper Sangria 139

Mason Jar Mojito   141

Pimm's Cup   143

Michelada   145

Whiskey Jam Cocktail   147

SNACKS IN A JAR   149

Roasted Garlic Parmesan Chickpeas   151

Ranch Hummus with Veggies   153

Bruschetta and Baguette Chips   155

Strawberry Jalapeño Salsa with
Cinnamon Sugar Pita Chips   157

Garlic Lemon Feta Dip with Pretzel Chips   159

Layered Dip with Tortilla Chips   161

DRESSINGS   163

Balsamic Vinaigrette   164

(Spicy Cilantro) Lime Vinaigrette   164

Honey-Lime Poppy Seed Dressing   164

White Wine Vinaigrette   164

Garlic Lemon Dijon Vinaigrette   164

Citrus Ginger Vinaigrette   165

Lemon Vinaigrette   165

Red Wine Vinaigrette   165

Apple Cider Vinaigrette   165

White Balsamic Vinaigrette   165

(Curry) Tahini Vinaigrette   166

(Chipotle) Creamy Avocado Dressing   166

Creamy BBQ Ranch Dressing   166

Spicy Peanut Dressing   166

Honey Lime Dressing   167

Creamy Pesto Dressing   167

IN GRATITUDE   169

INDEX   171

Mason Jar Lady

I arrived fashionably late to the mason jar party. As you may or may not know, I was traveling on the muffin pan bandwagon for many years. I even wrote a cookbook about it: *Do You Know the Muffin Pan?* I was the muffin pan lady for a long time, and that suited me. While muffin pans were my first love, when presented with the opportunity to learn about another out-of-the-box cooking tool, I was all for it.

Turns out, mason jars are also *totally* my thing. See, I have always loved anything self-contained. As a kid I loved kits. Any kind of kit! Art kits, makeup kits, stamp kits, DIY kits, even emergency kits. Everything you need for that task in one cute little box. As I got older, I started to make my own kits. I made traveling kits for my friends studying abroad, college dorm kits, thirtieth birthday kits, etc. Ask my sister—she receives a DIY kit every Christmas for our Christmas Crafternoon! It's her favorite thing in the world, I'm pretty sure. Maybe that's why I took to the mason jar so well. They are basically self-contained food kits. Everything you could need for breakfast, lunch, or picnics can be packed into a mason jar. The possibilities are endless.

Just like with the muffin pan cookbook, I searched in old cookbooks, menus, and on the glorious Internet to find inspiration for how to use the mason jar for cooking and eating. I had only scratched the surface of just how big mason jars were! I wasn't getting married, so I didn't search for mason jar centerpieces or table numbers. I wasn't a homeowner, so I didn't need to make mason jar lamps or soap dispensers. And with school and work and life, I certainly wasn't in the right state of mind to be thinking about turning mason jars into Halloween decorations. But now? Oh yeah, I'm considering it all!

I'd like you to think of this cookbook as your own personal "mason jar kit." Everything you'll need to explore and master the art of mason jars meals is in this cute little book. So, head out to your local grocery store, super store, or hardware store and pick up a mason jar or two . . . or eighty-seven. (Guilty!)

It's going to be Ah-Mason!
I hope you have a Ball!
It is o-Kerr-ing to me that this is getting out of hand.

All right, all right, I'm done.

Enjoy!
Amy

A Brief History of the Mason Jar

Mason jars have been around for more than 150 years, but the need for them goes back even further. In 1795, Napoleon Bonaparte offered a reward to anyone who could create a vessel that would preserve and carry food for troops that was also food safe and reliable. He inspired many to try and create something that had mass appeal. After a few failed attempts, finally, in 1858, John Mason patented his glass jar and zinc lid, calling it a "Mason Jar," revolutionizing the process of preserving food. Over time, Mason improved the seal of the jar, the downfall of his predecessors, and added the crucial rubber ring, making the seal more effective. However, in 1879 the patent for the Mason jar expired, allowing companies to create their own versions of the jar. Ball and Kerr rose to the challenge and became household names for mason jars and still hold that title today. While Ball was the first mass producer of the mason jar on the scene, Kerr was responsible for many of the modern additions to the jar that are still in place today. The company was responsible for adding the wide mouth opening and also the now-standard two-piece "dome lid."

While the mason jar was originally created for canning and preserving food over long periods of time, it offers an endless number of uses, including, but not limited to, creating delicious grab-and-go meals.

Mason Jar Salad Basics

Ingredients

Below is a handy list of the ingredients you will need to make the salads in this cookbook. It's also a quick-look list of ingredients to get the creative salad brain off and running. Use this list to create brand new salads with your favorite ingredients. Also, feel free to give that salad its own crazy name, like Beyoncé's Berry Barley Bonanza, and have fun with it!

Greens:
Mixed Greens
Arugula
Romaine
Kale
Spinach
Shaved Brussels Sprouts
Swiss Chard
Butter Lettuce

Veggies:
Cabbage
Broccoli
Asparagus
Cauliflower
Peas
Cherry Tomatoes
Butternut Squash
Sweet Potatoes
Corn
Jicama
Fennel
Onions
Peppers
Celery
Carrots
Bean Sprouts
Mushrooms
Cucumbers
Beets
Zucchini

Fruit:
Avocado
Mango
Apple
Watermelon
Peaches
Blueberries
Blackberries
Strawberries
Grapes
Pomegranate Seeds
Pineapple
Melon
Grapefruit
Kiwi
Oranges
Figs

Grains:
Quinoa
Rice
Pasta
Farro
Brown Rice

Protein:
Chicken
Fish
Steak
Prosciutto
Tofu
Egg

Shrimp
Chickpeas
Lentils
Black Beans
Edamame

Flavor Add-Ons:
Cilantro
Basil
Olives
Bacon
Green Onions
Shallots
Artichoke Hearts
Banana Peppers
Hearts of Palm
Dried Cranberries/Cherries
Pesto

Crunchy Toppings:
Tortilla Chips
Pita Chips
Popcorn
Croutons
Sunflower Seeds
Almonds
Walnuts
Radishes
Chia Seeds

Cheese:
Shredded Cheese
Blue Cheese
Feta
Goat Cheese
Parmesan
Mozzarella
Shaved Manchego
Cotija

Dressings
Oils:
Olive
Avocado
Walnut
Sesame

Peanut
Grapeseed

Acid/Vinegar:
Balsamic Vinegar
Red Wine Vinegar
White Wine Vinegar
Apple Cider Vinegar
Champagne Vinegar
Orange Vinegar
Rice Wine Vinegar
Lemon Juice
Lime Juice
Orange Juice

Flavor Boost:
Honey
Jam
Ginger
Mustard
Tahini
Soy Sauce
Garlic
Shallots
Sriracha
Sesame Seeds
Poppy Seeds
Cilantro
Minced Basil
Dried Oregano
Dill
Parsley
Mint
Thyme
Chives
Red Pepper Flakes
Parsley
Rosemary
Curry Powder

Emulsifier:
Hummus
Greek Yogurt
Ground Flax
Mustard
Mashed Avocado

Types of Jars

There are generally two types of **jars:** wide mouth and regular mouth, which refers to the jar's opening. A regular mouth jar is approximately 2⅜ inches wide, and the wide mouth measures approximately 3 inches.

   Mason jars come in a variety of sizes. Many are available in both wide mouth and regular, while some only come in one type, which I have researched and described here. I have also listed the ounces, cups, and typical uses for these jars. This can be used as a cheat sheet for deciding which jar to use.

Quart – 32 oz, 4 cups
wide and regular mouth
Best for: Salads

Pint and a half – 24 oz, 3 cups
wide mouth
Best for: Snacks

Pint – 16 oz, 2 cups
wide and regular mouth
Best for: Picnic in a jar, pasta and grain salads, drinks, or casseroles

Half Pint – 8 oz, 1 cup
wide and regular mouth
Best for: Dessert, jelly, jam, or pie in a jar

Quarter Pint – 4 oz, ½ cup
regular mouth
Best for: Dressings or toppings

Putting It Together

Greens:
To top it off.

Protein and Cheese:
This also includes toppings like nuts and croutons.

Soft Veggies:
Such as tomatoes, sweet potatoes, mushrooms, artichoke hearts, beets, etc.

Hearty Veggies:
Like cucumbers, chickpeas, beans, edamame, radishes, bell peppers, carrots, red onion, etc.

Dressing:
This goes on the bottom.

Useful Tools and Mason Jar Attachments

Some kitchen tools are essential in creating a variety of mason jar meals. Below are the tools that you will find particularly useful when making the recipes in this book.

Salad Spinner – If the lettuce isn't prewashed, a salad spinner is a great tool to make sure the lettuce stays very fresh.

Immersion Blender – This is the tool I use when making all of my smoothies. I put the immersion blender directly into the jar to blend. A word of caution: Use a slow speed when starting to blend in the jar in order to prevent ingredients from flying out of the jar. You can gradually increase the speed once the ingredients have started to combine.

Handheld Blender – A small countertop or handheld blender is used for making blended and creamy dressings. Also useful for chopping veggies or to make whipped topping.

Cuppow BNTO Cups – The Cuppow company has many great products that fit on or in mason jars. The BNTO is a plastic cup that fits inside the lid of the jar. You can fill the cup with dips, sauces, dressings, etc., to keep them separated from the food in the jar. It turns any jar into a lunch box!

Plastic Lids – I really like the option of using plastic lids. I don't worry about rust, and I know they are food safe. You can usually find them at your local home goods store.

Can Coozies – These are ideal for slipping over the outside of the warm or hot mason jar to keep your hands protected.

Cupcake Liners – Liners can be used to create layers within the mason jar. For example, when packing a Picnic in a Jar (see page 111) you can use a liner to separate the cookies from the crackers. A foil or parchment cupcake liner can be used in a pinch to hold dressing or toppings that need to be kept separated from the salad until it's time to serve.

Tips and Tricks

Below is a list of some of the lessons I learned about mason jars while writing this cookbook. Many are fairly obvious, while you may not have considered others. I hope that as you read through the list you are encouraged to dive headfirst into the wonderful world of mason jar meals.

- Mason jars are perfect for **making lunches** and picnic food ahead of time.
- They travel well in bags and lunch boxes. They are **airtight**, so they won't leak food.
- They can make **healthy living** convenient and quick to prepare.
- Most mason jars are dishwasher safe, but check the **labels** to be sure.
- Mason jars are food safe, make food look **fancy**, and take the guesswork out of what's inside!
- Metal lids should be hand washed and dried **immediately** to avoid rusting. They should be stored in an airtight container if possible.
- Salads with **avocados** should be prepared the night before you plan to eat them, or the morning of, and eaten within 12–14 hours of making the salad. Avocados brown quickly. Consider leaving the avocado out or bringing the whole avocado along to add to the salad before eating.
- Mason jars can be **very hot** after being microwaved. Remember to use your oven mitts or a can coozy to protect your hands.
- I recommend no more than 2 minutes for **reheating** items in the jar. Give the food a stir halfway through to ensure the whole jar is heated evenly.
- Most items prepared in a mason jar have a limited shelf life. After two days, I would check on the **freshness** of the food before eating it. Baked and cooked food will last a bit longer than the salads.
- Salads without **salad dressing** on the bottom will last longer in the fridge than those with dressing. If you're making a lot of salads in advance, consider leaving out the dressing so they stay good for the whole week.
- When creating mason jar salads, pack the food in **tight**. The less air in the jar the fresher the food stays.
- If the salad recipe has dressing on the bottom, allow the jar to sit out at **room temperature** for 1 or 2 minutes before serving. The cold air in the fridge may have made the oil thicker and therefore it will be harder to pour it out of the jar.
- I buy a lot of my food premade, such as **precut veggies**. With the salad-making process being so quick and easy, it helps me make more of them, which in turn keeps me eating a healthier diet.
- Make **big batches** of staple foods, like quinoa and roasted veggies, to use in salads and lunch dishes. Store the leftovers in the fridge in a mason jar.

How-To Recipes

Here are a few how-to recipes to get you rolling. These recipes make great staples for salads. Store them in mason jars for added cuteness.

Roasted Veggies

. . . .

As soon as I gather up my favorite veggies at the supermarket, I already start to feel healthier. As if buying the veggies will somehow make me also hit the gym and cut pizza out of my diet. I know this isn't true, I'm not that naive, but I am still so proud of myself for filling my cart with hearty veggies instead of copious amounts of chips and hummus. Once I get these miraculous veggies home, my favorite way to eat them is all roasted, crispy, and delicious. You can mix and match them according to your tastes and what's in season. Either way, this recipe will help you jump-start that healthy lifestyle, though I can't promise they'll keep the pizza and hummus at bay.

Ingredients:
brussels sprouts, halved
potato, cubed
cauliflower, chopped
pumpkin, cubed
butternut squash, cubed
sweet potato, cubed
broccoli, chopped
baby carrots
olive oil
salt and pepper, to taste
2 tbsp fresh or 1 tbsp dried rosemary or thyme, optional

Directions:
Preheat the oven to 425°F.

Place the veggies on a greased baking sheet. Lightly drizzle them with olive oil, then add salt, pepper, and herbs, if you choose. Give the veggies a quick stir to coat them with the oil.

Roast 15–18 minutes. Remove from the oven, then allow the veggies to cool before storing them in the fridge.

Candied Nuts

. . . .

I must warn you, once you make a tray of these candied nuts, you may have to quickly mix up a second batch or even a third. That's how fast these candied gems left my kitchen. The combination of spicy, sweet, and salty is incredibly hard to resist. Experiment with the spice. You may find yourself craving more spice than you thought you'd like. That's okay. I give you permission to make several batches to test them out. But remember, I warned you.

Ingredients:
½ cup brown sugar, packed
¼ cup granulated sugar
1 tsp salt
1 tbsp cinnamon
⅛ tsp cayenne
1 large egg white, whisked
1 tbsp water
4 cups (12 oz) raw walnuts, pecans, or almonds

Directions:
Preheat the oven to 300°F.

Put the sugars, salt, cinnamon, and cayenne into a resealable plastic bag. Seal the bag and shake vigorously until combined.

Combine the egg white and water in a bowl. Add the nuts and stir until evenly coated.

Add the nuts to the bag and shake until the nuts are coated with the cinnamon–sugar mixture.

Line a baking sheet with parchment paper and lay out a single layer of nuts. If they don't all fit on one sheet, use two.

Bake 40 minutes, stirring once halfway through. Remove from the oven and allow the candied nuts to cool until they've reached room temperature.

Store in an airtight container. A quart-size mason jar should hold a whole batch, save for a few that can conveniently be "taste tested."

Salads

Eating healthy isn't always easy. And, let's face it, sometimes it's not all that tasty. Getting greens and veggies into your daily routine is crucial for maintaining a healthy lifestyle, but with a hectic schedule it can be tough to turn down the quicker, less vitamin-rich options. This is where mason jar salads came in and save the day! They make eating healthy portable and convenient, since you can make them a couple days ahead of time.

Most of these salad recipes call for a layered approach, with the dressing safely on the bottom. The most popular way to eat a mason jar salad is to empty the jar into a bowl, letting the dressing cover the salad as you pour it. On occasion, I have been known to create a salad in a slightly larger jar than the recipe calls for and give that jar a shake to distribute the dressing. It's not only fun to shake the greens around, but it also saves on dishes; just one more time-saving featuring of the mason jar.

The possibilities for flavor combinations are endless. I encourage you to make substitutions based on your own dietary needs or what's in season. Take a lap around your local farmers' market; it's a great way to check out what's fresh and may open your eyes to new and interesting fruits and vegetables. Try a kumquat instead of blackberries, swap out arugula for watercress, experiment with Meyer lemons in everything. Another simple way to bring new life to a recipe is by changing the dressing. Try kombining spice with fruit and see how that suits you. Use a creamy dressing in place of a vinaigrette. Think of the following recipes as inspirations for your own personal salad masterpieces.

Taco Salad

Mason jar salads are not only beautiful, they're also convenient. I think this salad really brings out the beauty of what a mason jar salad can be: appealing to the eyes as well as the stomach. With this Mexican–inspired salad you get flavor, protein, and just enough spice to be a very satisfying lunch. If you're looking for an additional boost, I like to use roasted corn in this salad to give it more of a smoky flavor.

Jars: quart, wide mouth, and topping jar
Serves: 1

Ingredients:
2–3 tbsp (Spicy Cilantro) Lime Vinaigrette (see the recipe on page 164)
½ cup black beans
10–15 cherry or grape tomatoes, halved
½ cup corn kernels
½ avocado, diced
2 cups mixed greens
shredded Mexican cheese, to taste
green onions, chopped, to taste

Topping jar:
Handful of tortilla chips, crushed

Directions:
To assemble the salad, start with the desired amount of dressing, followed by the beans, then the tomatoes and corn. If you plan on eating the salad within the next few hours, place the avocado on top of the corn. If this salad is for taco Tuesday and it's Sunday, leave the avocado out until you're ready to eat. On top of the avocado or corn fill the jar with 2 cups of mixed greens. Top with the desired amount of cheese and green onions.

When you're ready to enjoy, pour the contents of the salad jar into a bowl then top with the crushed tortilla chips.

TIP: Don't want to carry around two jars? Use a cupcake liner or a piece of parchment paper at the top of the jar to hold the chips. Make sure the edge of the paper folds over the mouth of the jar before securing the lid.

Red, White, and Blueberry Balsamic Caprese

This is a very festive looking salad, perfect for celebrating the Fourth of July, Veterans Day, or any other time you're feeling patriotic. The use of blueberries in this traditional Italian caprese really brings out the sweetness of the balsamic vinegar.

Jars: pint, wide mouth
Serves: 2

Ingredients:
3 tbsp Balsamic Vinaigrette (see the recipe on page 164)
1½ cups cherry tomatoes
1 cup mozzarella ciliegine (cherry-size mozzarella)
1 cup blueberries
4 basil leaves, chiffonade

Directions:
Put all of the ingredients in a bowl and gently toss together. Divide the mixture into two pint jars. Once the salad is made, it should be served within 12 hours.

When you are ready to serve, pour the contents into a bowl or enjoy directly from the jar.

NOTE: If you plan to make this dish more than 12 hours in advance, keep the dressing on the side until you are ready to serve.

Strawberry, Avocado, and Kale Salad

Kale salads are so hot right now, and for good reason, since kale is packed full of vitamins. I really enjoy this kale salad in particular because of how well the toppings complement the kale. The combination of sweet strawberries, creamy avocado, and salty feta makes this salad a treat for your taste buds.

Jars: quart, wide mouth, and dressing jar
Serves: 1

Ingredients:
3–4 strawberries, diced
½ avocado, diced
3 cups kale
3 tbsp feta, crumbled
3 tbsp red onion, diced

Dressing jar:
Honey-Lime Poppy Seed Vinaigrette (see the recipe on page 164)

Directions:
To assemble the salad, start with a layer of diced strawberries on the bottom. On top of the strawberries add the avocado, and then tightly pack in 2 cups of kale. On top of the kale, sprinkle in the feta cheese and then add the red onion. Top with the remaining cup of kale.

When you are ready to enjoy, pour the salad into a bowl and top with the desired amount of dressing.

Guacamole Salad

This salad gives you all the deliciousness of guacamole, but deconstructed and served with a layer of hearty greens. All that's missing is a large bowl of freshly fried chips and a large margarita with salt on the side.

Jar: pint, wide mouth
Serves: 1

Ingredients:
2–3 tbsp (Spicy Cilantro) Lime Vinaigrette (see the recipe on page 164)
1 cup cherry tomatoes
¼ red onion, diced
½ avocado, diced
¼ cup cilantro
fresh-ground salt and pepper, to taste
2 cups mixed greens

Directions:
To assemble the salad, start with the spicy lime vinaigrette on the bottom. Next, add the tomatoes, followed by the red onion, the oh-so-important avocado, and then the cilantro. Crack some fresh salt and pepper on top before adding the mixed greens.

When you are ready to eat, pour the contents of the jar into a bowl and enjoy; the margarita is optional.

Arugula, Pear, and Gorgonzola Salad

This elegant salad may only have four ingredients, but it's full of flavor. If you want to impress your coworkers with your fancy salad skills, throw this salad together and say, "Oh, this ol' thing? Just some ingredients I had on hand. Why yes, I suppose it is really lovely. Thank you."

Jars: quart, wide mouth, and dressing jar
Serves: 1

Ingredients:
1 pear, diced (approx. 1 cup)
2 cups arugula
2 tbsp gorgonzola crumbles
2 tbsp pine nuts

Dressing jar:
White Wine Vinaigrette (see the recipe on page 164)

Directions:
To assemble the salad, place the ingredients in the jar starting with the diced pear followed by the arugula. Top the arugula layer with the gorgonzola crumbles and finish off with the pine nuts.

When you are ready to enjoy, pour the salad into a bowl and top with the desired amount of dressing.

Peach Caprese

This traditional tomato mozzarella layered caprese gets a sweet, summery twist with the addition of fresh peaches. This salad can be elevated even further if you seek out a high-quality mozzarella or, even more decadent, use burrata instead of mozzarella. Burrata is messier, however, so I recommend keeping the whole ball intact inside the jar. If peaches are not in season, strawberries, blueberries, or blackberries would be good substitutes.

Jar: pint, wide mouth
Serves: 1

Ingredients:
1 peach, sliced
1 large beefsteak or heirloom tomato, sliced
1 8-oz ball mozzarella, sliced
4–5 basil leaves

Directions:
Layer the slices in the jar, starting with a slice of peach, followed by a slice of tomato, then a mozzarella slice, and finally a basil leaf. Continue layering in the same order until there are no slices left.

When you are ready to eat, enjoy this dish directly from the jar, layer by tasty layer.

TIP: If eating a whole slice seems like too much of a mouthful, take a sharp knife and carefully cut the slices into quarters inside the jar.

Cranberry and Brussels Sprouts Salad

I can't think of a vegetable I like more than brussels sprouts. Roasted or raw, I could eat them every day. Luckily, it would be responsible of me if I did, because brussels sprouts are so good for you and a great source of vitamins C and K.

Jar: pint, wide mouth
Serves: 1

Ingredients:
2 cups brussels sprouts, shredded
2 tbsp dried cranberries
2 tbsp Parmesan cheese, shredded
2 tbsp sliced almonds

Dressing jar:
Garlic Lemon Dijon Vinaigrette (see the recipe on page 164)

Directions:
To assemble the salad, pack the brussel sprouts tightly into the jar. Top with dried cranberries, then add the Parmesan. Top with the sliced almonds.

When you are ready to enjoy, pour the salad into a bowl and top with the desired amount of dressing.

TIP: You can buy whole brussels sprouts and chop them yourself, but I prefer the already shredded version, because it makes creating healthy salads for lunch that much easier.

Chickpea, Avocado, and Kale Salad

After reading this recipe you might think to yourself, "Red pepper flakes and garlic powder, are you sure?" And I can say, with a full stomach, "Yes, I am very sure." The surprise of the spice and the boost of garlic flavor have made this one of my new favorite dishes to have for dinner.

Jar: quart, wide mouth
Serves: 1

Ingredients:
2–3 tbsp White Wine Vinaigrette (see the recipe on page 164)
½ cup chickpeas
¼ cup red onions, diced
½ avocado, diced
½ tsp garlic powder
red pepper flakes, to taste
2 cups kale

Directions:
To assemble the salad, place the ingredients in the jar, starting with the White Wine Vinaigrette. Follow the vinaigrette with the chickpeas, then the red onions. Add the avocado, then season the salad with the garlic powder and red pepper flakes. Top with the 2 cups of kale.

When you are ready to eat, pour the contents of the jar into a bowl and enjoy.

Watermelon, Feta, and Arugula Salad

Nothing says summer like sweet, juicy watermelon. This salad is surprisingly elegant and would make an excellent side dish at a barbecue. To give this dish a little Mexican flair, try this salad with the (Spicy Cilantro) Lime Vinaigrette, watermelon, cotija cheese, and cilantro.

Jar: quart, wide mouth
Serves: 1

Ingredients:
2–3 tbsp White Wine Vinaigrette (see the recipe on page 164)
1 cup seedless watermelon, cubed
1 tbsp feta, crumbled or cubed
1 tbsp sliced almonds
4 mint leaves, torn
2 cups arugula

Directions:
To start, pour the desired amount of white wine vinaigrette into the jar. Gently place the watermelon on top of the vinaigrette. Sprinkle in the feta cheese and almonds. Add the mint, then pack the rest of the jar full with the arugula.

When you are ready to eat, carefully pour the contents of the jar into a bowl and enjoy.

Roasted Fall Salad

Like the title suggests, this salad provides a nice little taste of fall. I like to buy my pepitas already prepared for this salad, but you can make them yourself at home and add your own creative combination of spices. This dish would also be great served over brown rice or barley.

Jar: pint, wide mouth
Serves: 1

Ingredients:
1–2 tbsp Balsamic Vinaigrette (see the recipe on page 164)
¾ cup butternut squash, roasted and cooled
¾ cup brussels sprouts, roasted and cooled
2 tbsp pomegranate seeds
1 tbsp pepitas (pumpkin seeds)
½ cup kale, raw or steamed

Directions:
To assemble the salad, start with the vinaigrette on the bottom of the jar. Layer in the roasted butternut squash first, followed by the brussels sprouts. Next up, add the pomegranate seeds and pepitas. Finally, top the whole dish with the kale.

When you are ready to eat, pour the contents of the jar into a bowl and enjoy.

BBQ Chicken Salad

. . . .

The tangy BBQ sauce combined with the familiar flavor of ranch dressing is what makes this salad so good. If you want to add more veggies, chickpeas and bell peppers would be great additions to this salad. The only thing that would make this salad any better for me is if a handsome cowboy rode up and delivered it to me, personally, at work.

Jar: quart, wide mouth
Serves: 1

Ingredients:
2–3 tbsp Creamy BBQ Ranch Dressing (see the recipe on page 166)
½ cup black beans, drained
¼ cup corn kernels
¼ cup cucumber, diced
⅓ cup tomato, chopped
½–1 cup chicken, cooked and cubed
2 tbsp green onions
banana peppers, to taste
2 tbsp cheddar cheese, shredded
2 cups romaine lettuce, chopped

Directions:
To assemble the salad, lay down a base of the dressing. The next layer is the black beans, followed by the corn, cucumber, and tomato. Next up, add a layer of chicken and then the green onions. Put in the desired amount of banana peppers and top with the cheddar cheese. Finally, fill the jar with the romaine.

When you are ready to eat, pour the contents of the jar into a bowl and enjoy.

Asian Pear and Cashew Salad

I took a step off the usual path when I created this salad, but it contains some great unique ingredients. Like a family, every ingredient in this salad is good on its own, but together they make a great salad team. If Asian pears and bean sprouts aren't readily available, regular pears and watercress or alfalfa are great substitutes.

Jar: quart, wide mouth
Serves: 1

Ingredients:
2–3 tbsp Citrus Ginger Vinaigrette (see the recipe on page 165)
½ cup red bell pepper, chopped
½ stalk of celery, chopped
1 Asian pear, diced
½ cup bean sprouts
¼ cup roasted cashews
2 basil leaves, chiffonade
1 cup arugula

Directions:
To assemble the salad, start with a generous layer of the vinaigrette. Next up, add the bell pepper, followed by the celery. Cover with the diced pear and then add the bean sprouts. Drop in the cashews and basil. Finally, top off the jar with the arugula.

When you are ready to eat, pour the contents of the jar into a bowl and enjoy.

Mango, Strawberry, and Arugula Salad

This salad is so sweet and colorful. I love the combination of mango and goat cheese. The creamy goat cheese really complements the tart mango, and with the addition of sweet strawberries and bitter arugula, this is a very dynamic salad.

Jars: quart, wide mouth, and dressing jar
Serves: 1

Ingredients:
2–3 tbsp red onion, diced
½ small mango, cubed
4–5 strawberries, sliced
½ avocado, cubed
goat cheese, crumbled, to taste
2 cups arugula

Dressing jar:
(Spicy Cilantro) Lime Vinaigrette (see the recipe on page 164)

Directions:
To assemble the salad, lay down a base of chopped red onion in the jar. Next up is the mango, followed by the strawberries and then the avocado. Top with the crumbled goat cheese. Finally, fill the jar with arugula.

When you are ready to enjoy, pour the salad into a bowl and top with the desired amount of dressing.

My Big Fat Greek Salad

I know, I know, it's an old joke, but like this salad, it's a goody. To mix things up a bit I added orzo, which really makes this salad both beautiful and filling.

Jar: quart, wide mouth
Serves: 1

Ingredients:
2–3 tbsp Lemon Vinaigrette (see the recipe on page 165)
½ zucchini, chopped
½ cup chickpeas
½ cup orzo
2 tbsp kalamata olives, chopped
3 tbsp red onions, diced
⅓ cup cherry tomatoes, halved
2–3 tbsp feta cheese
1 cup spinach
pine nuts, to taste

Directions:
To assemble the salad, place the ingredients in the jar starting with the vinaigrette. Then add the zucchini, followed by the chickpeas and orzo. Add the chopped olives and red onions. Carefully add a layer of cherry tomatoes and top them with the feta. Pack in the spinach and finish it off with the pine nuts.

When you are ready to eat, pour the contents of the jar into a bowl and enjoy.

Pear, Pomegranate, and Spinach Salad

This is such a festive looking salad, not to mention delicious. The red and green makes it the perfect lunch to pack around the holidays. And since our lives are busy enough, especially around the holidays, I recommend buying pomegranate arils already removed. This not only saves time, but it also keeps your hands from turning a festive shade of red.

Jars: quart, wide mouth, and dressing jar
Serves: 1

Ingredients:
½ pear, diced
⅓ cup pomegranate arils
2–3 tbsp dried cranberries
⅓ cup toasted pecans, chopped
2–3 tbsp goat cheese
2 cups baby spinach

Dressing jar:
White Wine Vinaigrette (see the recipe on page 164)

Directions:
To assemble the salad, start by adding the diced pear into the jar, followed by the pomegranate arils. Next, add the dried cranberries followed by a layer of pecans. Sprinkle on the goat cheese and finish with the baby spinach.

When you are ready to enjoy, pour the salad into a bowl and top with the desired amount of dressing.

Mexican Avocado Caesar Salad

Casear salad is one the most recognizable salads, and it can be found on the menu at most Italian restaurants, but the Caesar salad actually originated in Mexico. Who knew? So, in honor of its origins, this salad has been given a bit of Mexican flair by adding avocado to the dressing and pepitas and cotija cheese to the salad. Buen apetito!

Jar: quart, wide mouth
Serves: 1

Ingredients:
2–3 tbsp (Chipotle) Creamy Avocado Dressing (see the recipe on page 166)
½ cup cherry tomatoes, halved
3 oz grilled chicken, optional
¼ avocado, cubed
1–2 tbsp cotija cheese, crumbled
1 tbsp pepitas
2 cups kale

Directions:
To assemble this salad, start with the dressing in the bottom of the jar. Add the tomatoes, then layer in the chicken followed by the avocado. Next, sprinkle on the cheese and pepitas, and then top with some fresh, crispy kale.

When you are ready to eat, pour the contents of the jar into a bowl and enjoy. *Que rico!*

Peach, Blueberry, and Feta Salad

· ·

I really enjoy this salad with its combination of sweet fruit and salty feta. It is so summery and fresh that it begs to be eaten outdoors under a clear blue sky. If peaches aren't in season, you can substitute frozen peaches. Just add the frozen fruit to the jar and allow it to thaw, with the rest of the salad, overnight in the refrigerator.

Jars: quart, wide mouth, and dressing jar
Serves: 1

Ingredients:
½ peach, chopped
½ cup blueberries
2 tbsp feta
2 tbsp red onion, diced
⅓ cup candied pecans (see the recipe on page xxi)
2 cups mixed greens

Dressing jar:
White Balsamic Vinaigrette (see the recipe on page 165)

Directions:
To assemble the salad, start with the fruit, putting the peach in first then the blueberries. Sprinkle in the feta, then add the onion and pecans. Finish off the jar with the mixed greens.

When you are ready to eat, pour the contents of the jar into a bowl, top with the desired amount of dressing, and enjoy.

Chinese Chicken Salad

I know my parents are very proud of me, no matter what crazy project I'm trying, and this cookbook was no exception. They were very excited about this project in particular because of all the new and different healthy salads they got to try during the testing process. But I made sure not to miss my mama's favorite salad. Just like her, I know you'll want to devour this sweet, tangy, crunchy salad and not share it with anyone.

Jar: quart, wide mouth
Serves: 1

Ingredients:
2–3 tbsp Citrus Ginger Vinaigrette (see the recipe on page 165)
¼ cup carrots, shredded
½ cup edamame beans
3 oz or 1 cup chicken, cooked and diced
1 tbsp green onion, thinly sliced
1 mandarin orange, peeled and broken into segments (can substitute canned)
1 tbsp almond slices
2 cups romaine

Directions:
Add the vinaigrette to the jar first. Top with the carrot, then the edamame, followed by the chicken. Next up, add the green onion and the mandarin orange segments. Sprinkle in the almonds and top with the romaine.

When you are ready to eat, pour the contents of the jar into a bowl and enjoy.

Curry Butternut Squash Salad

. . . .

Autumn is my favorite time of year. The colors, the crisp air, scarves—everything about the season calls me outside to appreciate its beauty. When I'm not walking around and enjoying the scenery, you can usually find me inside, making soup or roasting veggies. There's something about roasted butternut squash or pumpkin (or any roasted vegetables for that matter) that makes me fall for fall. I think this salad would be a perfect lunch to make around Thanksgiving time. I picture it paired with some delicious turkey and, ideally, a nap.

Jar: quart, wide mouth
Serves: 1

Ingredients:
2–3 tbsp (Curry) Tahini Vinaigrette (see the recipe on page 166)
½ cup chickpeas
1 cup butternut squash, cooked and diced
1–2 tbsp cilantro
candied pecans, to taste (see the recipe on page xxi)
2 cups kale

Directions:
To make the salad, first add the vinaigrette to the jar. Next, layer in the chickpeas followed by the squash. Add the cilantro and then toss in the candied pecans. Top the jar off with the kale.

When you are ready to eat, pour the contents of the jar into a bowl and enjoy.

Prosciutto, Melon, and Arugula Salad

This salad is a crowd-pleaser, which is unfortunate since it only serves one. If you're feeling generous—and I always support being generous—I encourage making several of these salad jars for any party where you'd like the guests to be very pleased. The combination of prosciutto and melon is the ideal marriage of salty and sweet. Add to that the bitterness of arugula and the creamy mozzarella and you've got a dynamic, sophisticated salad.

Jar: pint, wide mouth
Serves: 1

Ingredients:
2 tbsp White Balsamic Vinaigrette (see the recipe on page 165)
1 cup cantaloupe, cubed or balled
3 slices prosciutto, cut into pieces
½ cup mozzarella ciliegine
1½ cups arugula

Directions:
To assemble the salad, first add the vinaigrette to the jar. Then place the cantaloupe in the jar and top with pieces of the prosciutto. Add in the mozzarella, and then fill the remaining space in the jar with arugula.

When you are ready to eat, pour the contents of the jar into a bowl and enjoy.

5 B Salad

Brussels sprouts, blackberries, blue cheese, bacon, and balsamic dressing make up the five Bs of this salad. While brussels sprouts are great raw, they also taste fantastic roasted. Try roasting them (see the recipe for Roasted Veggies on page xix) for this salad to add a whole new layer of flavor.

Jars: quart, wide mouth, and dressing jar
Serves: 1

Ingredients:
2 cups brussels sprouts, shredded
1 cup blackberries
2 slices bacon, cooked and crumbled
2 tbsp blue cheese, crumbled

Dressing jar:
Balsamic Vinaigrette (see the recipe on page 164)

Directions:
This salad is layered a little differently than the other salads in this book. In order to keep the brussels sprouts from squishing the blackberries, and because they can take the weight, we start with the brussels sprouts on the bottom. On top of the sprouts, add the blackberries, and then top the salad off with the bacon and blue cheese crumbles.

When you are ready to enjoy, pour the salad into a bowl and top with the desired amount of dressing.

Chipotle Sweet Potato, Black Bean, and Kale Salad

I'm a firm believer that inspiration is everywhere. This salad is inspired by a really great veggie burger I had recently. I loved the combination of black beans and sweet potatoes in the patty. The burger was topped with avocado and a creamy chipotle spread. It was so great that I took some time and deconstructed it into a salad.

Jar: quart, wide mouth
Serves: 1

Ingredients:
2 tbsp (Chipotle) Creamy Avocado Dressing (see the recipe on page 166)
½ cup black beans, drained
1 cup sweet potato, roasted and cubed
¼ avocado, cubed
2 cups kale

Directions:
To assemble this salad, start with the chipotle avocado dressing on the bottom of the jar. To that, add the black beans, followed by the roasted sweet potato, and then the avocado. Fill the jar up with the kale.

When you are ready to eat, pour the contents of the jar into a bowl and enjoy.

Honeycrisp and Spinach Salad

The colors of this salad are bright and inviting. The dried cranberries and blue cheese combination provides a great one-two punch of sweet and savory. Of course, any apple variety would work in this salad, but since Honeycrisp are my favorite kind of apple they get their very own salad.

Jar: quart, wide mouth, and dressing jar
Serves: 1

Ingredients:
½ Honeycrisp apple, sliced
2–3 tbsp dried cranberries
2 cups spinach
1–2 tbsp blue cheese, crumbled
candied walnuts, chopped, to taste (see the recipe on page xxi)

Dressing jar:
Apple Cider Vinaigrette (see the recipe on page 165)

Directions:
To create this salad, start by putting the apple slices into the bottom of the jar. Sprinkle in the dried cranberries then add the spinach. Top the salad with blue cheese crumbles and the candied walnuts.

When you are ready to enjoy, pour the salad into a bowl and top with the desired amount of dressing.

Steak House Salad

This is another salad with very few ingredients but really great flavor. Butter lettuce is such a light, delicate green, but it complements the steak really well. I also enjoy the addition of corn, because it provides a little sweetness to the salad.

Jar: quart, wide mouth
Serves: 1

Ingredients:
2 tbsp White Wine Vinaigrette (see the recipe on page 164)
⅔ cup corn kernels
2–3 oz steak, cooked to taste and thinly sliced
1 green onion, chopped
2 cups butter lettuce, torn into pieces
1–2 tbsp blue cheese, crumbled

Directions:
Start to build this salad with the vinaigrette as a foundation. Next, layer in the corn and then the steak. Top with the green onion and cover with the lettuce. Sprinkle the blue cheese crumbles over the rest of the ingredients.

When you are ready to eat, pour the contents of the jar into a bowl and enjoy.

Antipasto Salad with Mixed Greens

I put a lot of thought into this recipe. I enlisted the help of my Uncle Carl and his family to help me come up with this one. They are the antipasto experts. Together we created a salad recipe that is delicious and very Italian. The ingredients in this salad would also work really well as a picnic appetizer or in a pasta salad.

Jar: quart, wide mouth
Serves: 1

Ingredients:
1–2 tbsp Red Wine Vinaigrette (see the recipe on page 165)
¼ cup marinated artichokes, chopped
½ cup mozzarella ciliegine, halved
¼ cup roasted red peppers, diced
3 large green olives, chopped
¼ cup Genoa salami, small slices or cubed
2 cups mixed greens

Directions:
Start assembly by putting the vinaigrette into the jar. Add in the artichokes, and then the mozzarella. The red peppers come next, followed by the chopped olives. Place the salami in the jar, and then finish with the greens.

When you are ready to eat, pour the contents of the jar into a bowl and enjoy.

Rainbow Salad

This salad is as delicious as it is colorful. It's also known as the "Clean Out Your Fridge Salad," but "Rainbow Salad" sounds far more appetizing. I encourage you to experiment with different dressings for this one—for example, the Creamy Pesto Dressing would also be really delicious in this salad.

Jar: quart, wide mouth
Serves: 1

Ingredients:
2–3 tbsp (Chipotle) Creamy Avocado Dressing (see the recipe on page 166)
½ cup tomato, chopped
½ cup carrot, chopped
½ cup yellow bell pepper, chopped
½ cup cucumber, diced
½ cup kidney beans
½ cup purple cabbage, shredded

Directions:
To assemble the salad, start with the dressing. Next, put in a layer of tomato and then carrot, with the bell pepper on top. Add the diced cucumber and kidney beans, and then finish filling the jar with the shredded purple cabbage.

When you are ready to eat, pour the contents of the jar into a bowl and enjoy.

Mediterranean Artichoke and Spinach Salad

This salad is so fresh and lemony. If you want to make this into a dinner-size salad, as I often do, you can add rotisserie chicken or seasoned ground turkey. Once again, if you're feeling more like eating pasta and less like eating a salad (and no judgments here if you do) this salad would taste great with some orzo or mini shell pasta.

Jar: quart, wide mouth
Serves: 1

Ingredients:
2 tbsp Lemon Vinaigrette (see the recipe on page 165)
½ cup cucumber, diced
3 tbsp red onion, chopped
½ cup marinated artichokes
½ cup tomatoes, diced
feta, crumbled, to taste
2 cups spinach

Directions:
Add the vinaigrette to the jar first. Then add the cucumber and red onion. Toss the artichokes into the jar, followed by the tomatoes. Top those off with the feta. Lastly, layer in the spinach to fill the jar.

When you are ready to eat, pour the contents of the jar into a bowl and enjoy.

Tropical Chicken Salad

First, close your eyes and imagine you're lying on a white sand beach (fruity drink complete with umbrella optional). Next to you sits a salad, beautiful and spicy, layered with sweet pineapple, bright red tomatoes, and creamy avocado. The troubles of the working world are far behind you. Now, open your eyes. If you're not on some beach with a drink in hand, I'm sorry, but you still have this great salad.

Jar: quart, wide mouth
Serves: 1

Ingredients:
2–3 tbsp (Spicy Cilantro) Lime Vinaigrette (see the recipe on page 164)
½ cup pineapple or mango, diced
¼ cup tomato, chopped
1 cup chicken, cooked and diced or shredded
¼ cup red onion, chopped
½ avocado, diced
2 cups spinach

Directions:
Kick-start this salad with the spicy vinaigrette in the bottom of the jar. Next, add in the sweetness of the fruit. The bright red of the tomato comes next, followed by the chicken and onion. The creamy avocado follows close behind, with the spinach layered on top.

When you are ready to eat, pour the contents of the jar into a bowl and enjoy.

Strawberry, Goat Cheese, and Spinach Salad

This recipe is inspired by a salad my grad school roommate used to make all the time. She called it "Summer Salad." It was such a nice change from the steady diet of cold turkey sandwiches and chips I ate every day. It brings back great memories. This is probably the reason why I make this salad more than any other recipe in this cookbook.

I always have goat cheese on hand, so when I find really fresh bright red strawberries I gather up the rest of the ingredients to create this easy, delicious salad.

Jar: quart, wide mouth, and dressing jar
Serves: 1

Ingredients:
1 cup strawberries, diced or sliced
2 tbsp red onion, diced
2 cups spinach
1–2 tbsp goat cheese
2 tbsp walnuts, toasted

Dressing jar:
White Balsamic Vinaigrette (see the recipe on page 165)

Directions:
To assemble the salad, start with a layer of strawberries on the bottom of the jar. Toss the red onions on top, followed by the spinach. Finally, sprinkle the goat cheese and walnuts on top.

When you are ready to enjoy, pour the salad into a bowl and top with the desired amount of dressing.

Broccoli, Almond, and Cherry Salad

I know the first word in this salad is broccoli, which for some may sound scary. But don't worry, because what you don't see in the title is that this salad also has a good-sized portion of bacon in it as well—and everything is better with bacon, even broccoli. Unless, of course, you're a vegetarian and maybe you love broccoli, then in that case, take out the bacon and enjoy the classic combination of almonds and cherries in this broccoli salad.

Jars: pint, wide mouth
Serves: 2

Ingredients:
3 tbsp Lemon Vinaigrette (see the recipe on page 165)
2–3 tbsp plain Greek yogurt
2 cups broccoli, chopped
¼ cup red onion, chopped
¼ cup dried cherries
2 strips of bacon, cooked and crumbled
¼ cup almonds, chopped or slivered

Directions:
First, whisk together the vinaigrette and yogurt in a medium bowl. To this mixture, add the broccoli, red onion, dried cherries, and crumbled bacon. Stir to combine. Gently fold in the almonds. Distribute the broccoli salad evenly between two jars.

When you are ready to eat, pour the contents into a bowl or enjoy directly from the jar.

Zucchini Noodle Salad

Zucchini noodles! Who knew? I loved making these healthy noodles, or "zoodles," as they are often affectionately called. They are quickly becoming a big hit at my house. The edamame and pesto dressing really complements this salad.

Jar: quart, wide mouth
Serves: 1

Ingredients:
2–3 tbsp Creamy Pesto Dressing (see the recipe on page 167)
3 cups zucchini noodles
½ cup edamame, shelled
½ cup red bell pepper, diced
½ cup cherry tomatoes, halved
¼ cup feta, crumbled
2 tbsp olives, chopped

Directions:
To assemble the salad, start by adding the dressing to the jar. Next up come the zucchini noodles, followed by the bell pepper. Then, add the edamame and cherry tomatoes. Sprinkle in the feta and add the chopped olives. Finish the salad off with more zucchini noodles if desired.

When you are ready to enjoy, pour the contents of the jar into a bowl, then stir to evenly distribute the dressing.

Orzo, Spinach, and Sun-Dried Tomato Salad

I have become somewhat of a picnic aficionado recently. I live several blocks away from a very beautiful park in San Francisco. Carrying a picnic basket filled with mason jars, I walk the short distance to the park and enjoy the sunshine and gorgeous view of the city as often as I can. This salad is great to take on a picnic, especially with some grilled chicken breasts and white wine. Actually, that sounds wonderful. I'll be back in a little bit!

Jars: pint, wide mouth
Serves: 2

Ingredients:
3–4 tbsp Lemon Vinaigrette (see the recipe on page 165)
1 cup orzo pasta, cooked
¼ cup feta, crumbled or cubed
¼ cup kalamata olives
¼ cup red onion, diced
¼ cup sun-dried tomatoes, slivered
1 cup fresh spinach, chopped

Directions:
To assemble each salad, start with a tablespoon or two of vinaigrette in each jar. Then, split the cup of orzo between the two jars. Next, layer in half the feta, olives, red onion, and tomatoes into each jar. Top each jar with ½ cup of spinach.

When you are ready to eat, pour the contents into two bowls or enjoy directly from the jar.

Mexican Corn Salad

There are very few foods I'm a not crazy about. I know it seems odd to mention, but corn is on that short list. My sister, however, adores corn. So, I tried to create a recipe that we both could really enjoy. This is that dish! Spicy corn with Greek yogurt and green chilies; that is corn I can really get behind.

Jar: pint, wide mouth
Serves: 1

Ingredients:
2–3 tbsp (Spicy Cilantro) Lime Vinaigrette (see the recipe on page 164)
1½ cups sweet corn
2 tbsp plain Greek yogurt
1 tbsp diced chilies
1 tsp chili powder
2 tbsp cotija cheese
1 tbsp cilantro, chopped
½ green onion, chopped

Directions:
Put all the ingredients into a small bowl and stir well to combine. Then, put the salad into a jar.

When you are ready to eat, pour the contents into a bowl or enjoy directly from the jar.

Sweet Potato and Chickpea Salad

I made a promise to a good family friend, Anaperla, that I would include at least one vegetarian and one vegan salad in this cookbook. Vegetarian salads are easy to do, only a handful call for chicken or turkey, and one or two have steak. But vegan? That was more difficult for me. I really, really like cheese and put it in almost everything I eat, especially salad. But I'm flexible, and if it's important to those I care about, it's important to me too. So Anaperla, this recipe is dedicated to you. I hope you enjoy it.

Jar: quart, wide mouth
Serves: 1

Ingredients:
2–3 tbsp (Curry) Tahini Vinaigrette (see the recipe on page 166)
½ cup chickpeas
½ cup cherry tomatoes, halved
2 tbsp red onion, diced
1 cup sweet potato, roasted and cubed
1 tbsp cilantro
2 cups kale

Directions:
To assemble the salad, start with a nice layer of the vinaigrette in the jar. Next, add a generous layer of chickpeas. On top of the chickpeas add the tomatoes, diced red onions, and the oh-so-important roasted sweet potato. Sprinkle in the cilantro and top the whole salad off with a generous portion of hearty kale.

When you are ready to eat, pour the contents of the jar into a bowl and enjoy.

Zucchini, Corn, and Quinoa Salad

This is a healthy 10-minute side dish that will dress up any meal. It is simple, yet full of flavor! This salad would be another great picnic side dish when served alongside grilled chicken or spinach and turkey meatballs.

Jar: pint, wide mouth
Serves: 1

Ingredients:
2 tbsp (Spicy Cilantro) Lime Vinaigrette (see the recipe on page 164)
½ cup zucchini, chopped
1 cup corn
½ cup quinoa, cooked
¼ cup cherry tomatoes, halved
2 tbsp cilantro, roughly chopped
2 tbsp Parmesan, grated or shaved

Directions:
To assemble the salad, start with the vinaigrette on the bottom of the jar. A layer of zucchini comes next, followed by the corn. Next, carefully add the quinoa and then top with the cherry tomatoes and cilantro. Finish the salad off with the Parmesan.

When you are ready to eat, pour the contents into a bowl or enjoy directly from the jar.

Avocado and White Bean Salad

This bean salad gets better the more time it is given to sit in the refrigerator and soak up all that great Garlic Lemon Dijon Vinaigrette. But don't wait too long, because this dish is so delicious. The recipe serves two, so take this bean salad, along with a nice crusty loaf of bread and some white wine, to the park and share with a friend.

Jars: pint, wide mouth
Serves: 2

Ingredients:
2–3 tbsp Garlic Lemon Dijon Vinaigrette (see the recipe on page 164)
1 avocado, diced
1 15-oz can cannellini beans, drained
1 Roma tomato, chopped
¼ sweet onion, diced

Directions:
Combine all of the ingredients in a medium bowl. Gently stir until the avocado, beans, tomato, and onion are thoroughly coated in the vinaigrette.

Divide the mixture into the two jars.

When you are ready to eat, pour the contents into a bowl or enjoy directly from the jar.

Honey and Peach Panzanella

Panzanella is a popular rustic Italian salad that's made using leftover or day-old bread. Traditionally, the salad consists of hearty bread cut into cubes, tomatoes, basil, and olive oil—simple yet satisfying. In this recipe the salad is dressed up a bit by the addition of peaches and mozzarella cheese.

Jar: pint, wide mouth
Serves: 1

Ingredients:
1–2 tbsp olive oil, for toasting bread
½ cup hearty bread, cubed
2–3 tbsp Balsamic Vinaigrette (see the recipe on page 164)
1 tbsp honey
1 peach, diced
½ cup grape tomatoes, halved
½ cup mozzarella ciliegine
3 mint or basil leaves, chiffonade

Directions:
Heat the olive oil in a skillet over medium heat then add the bread cubes. Turn the cubes several times to toast all sides. Allow the bread to cool slightly before putting the panzanella together. To assemble the salad, start by putting the vinaigrette in the bottom of the jar. Pour in the honey. Next, add the diced peaches followed by the tomatoes. Put in the mozzarella, and then top with the mint or basil. Top off the jar with the toasted bread cubes.

When you are ready to eat, pour the contents of the jar into a bowl and enjoy.

Buffalo Chicken and Quinoa Salad

This salad is everything you love about buffalo wings, but in a salad. It's also very versatile. By eliminating the quinoa and replacing the greens with a cup of pasta shells, you have a delicious buffalo chicken pasta salad.

Jar: quart, wide mouth
Serves: 1

Ingredients:
½ cup chicken, cooked and shredded or cubed
¼ cup buffalo sauce
2 tbsp sour cream
½ cup quinoa, cooked
2 tbsp red onion, diced
¼ cup celery, chopped thinly
¼ cup sweet corn
¼ cup cherry tomatoes, halved
2 tbsp cilantro
blue cheese, crumbled, to taste
1 cup mixed greens

Directions:
In a small bowl, combine the chicken, buffalo sauce, and sour cream. Stir until the chicken is coated. To assemble the salad, lay down a base of cooked quinoa followed by the diced red onions. Next, add a layer of the buffalo chicken. Drop in the chopped celery, then the corn and tomatoes. Sprinkle in the cilantro and blue cheese. Finally, top the whole salad with the mixed greens.

When you are ready to eat, pour the contents of the jar into a bowl and enjoy.

Bacon and Pea Pasta Salad

If your family or friends are anything like mine, this salad will be a dish everyone fights over. Since the first time I tested this recipe out, I've had requests to make it at least once every few weeks. That's how good it is. All the talk about this salad has me tempted to mix up a batch right now. Excuse me, I'll be right back.

Jars: pint, wide mouth
Serves: 2

Ingredients:
¼ cup bacon, cooked and crumbled
1 cup peas
½ cup cheddar, shredded
1½ cups small pasta shells, cooked
¼ cup red onion, diced
½ cup plain Greek yogurt
¼ tsp paprika
salt and pepper, to taste

Directions:
Place all of the ingredients in a small bowl and stir to combine. Distribute the salad evenly into two jars.

When you are ready to eat, pour the contents into two bowls or enjoy directly from the jars.

Thai Peanut Pasta Salad

This is a mason jar–friendly version of my favorite pasta salad from Trader Joe's. I love the combination of spicy sriracha and peanut butter in the dressing. Split between two jars, this is the perfect pack-and-go romantic picnic for two. You will really impress your date with this one, or you can bring the extra one to work to share with a coworker or crush. You'll be their new favorite person.

Jars: pint, wide mouth
Serves: 2

Ingredients:
4 tbsp Spicy Peanut Dressing (see the recipe on page 166)
1 cup chicken, cooked and cubed
2 cups cooked spaghetti noodles
½ cup red bell pepper, chopped
¼ cup cilantro, chopped
2 green onions, chopped
1 cup purple cabbage, shredded
½ cup carrots, shredded
peanuts, to taste

Directions:
To assemble the salads, start by pouring 2 tablespoons of the peanut dressing into each of the jars. Split the remaining ingredients, putting half into each jar, starting with the chicken. Next, add the noodles followed by the bell pepper. Spice it up with the cilantro. Then add a layer each of the green onions, cabbage, and carrots. Top each jar with peanuts.

When you are ready to eat, pour the contents of the jar into two bowls and enjoy.

Fruit Salad

For this recipe, I suggest using whatever fresh fruit is in season. If possible, ensure that you have fruit in a variety of colors, so your fruit salad looks as good as it tastes. This recipe is just one suggestion for creating a palate–pleasing fruit salad—the possibilities are endless.

Jars: pint, wide mouth, and dressing jar
Serves: 2

Ingredients:
1 kiwi, sliced
1 cup blueberries
1 cup fresh pineapple, cubed
1 tangerine, peeled and segmented
1 cup strawberries, sliced
1 peach, diced
1 cup blackberries

Dressing jar:
Honey Lime Dressing (see the recipe on page 167)

Directions:
Layer the ingredients into the two jars in the same order as they're listed above, starting with the kiwi, and topping the jars off with the blackberries.

When you are ready to eat, pour the contents of the jar into two bowls, and then drizzle with the desired amount of the Honey Lime Dressing. Simply sweet and delicious.

Overnight Refrigerator Oats

Getting out the door in the morning just got a whole lot easier with these overnight refrigerator oats. Once you layer the ingredients in the jar, the fridge takes over and does all the work for you while you sleep. Imagine if other chores were taken care of this easily, how simple life would be. If the laundry could move itself from the washer to the dryer, or the dishwasher would unload itself, we'd have so much more time to enjoy life. Until those things become a reality, you can make up to three days' worth of these recipes ahead of time and enjoy an easy on-the-go breakfast.

Jar: Pint
Serves: 1

Basic Refrigerator Oats
Ingredients:
⅓ cup old-fashioned or rolled oats
⅓ cup unsweetened almond/coconut/ skim/ whole milk
½ cup plain low-fat Greek yogurt
1½ tsp chia seeds, optional
1 tsp honey, optional

Piña Colada Refrigerator Oats
Ingredients:
⅓ cup old-fashioned or rolled oats
⅓ cup coconut milk
½ cup coconut flavor Greek yogurt
½ cup pineapple, chopped
Topping: shredded coconut

Key Lime Pie Refrigerator Oats
Ingredients:
⅓ cup old-fashioned or rolled oats
⅓ cup almond milk or coconut milk
½ cup vanilla or plain Greek yogurt
½ tsp lime zest
Juice of 1 key lime
pinch of salt
Topping: crushed graham crackers

Triple Berry Refrigerator Oats
Ingredients:
⅓ cup old-fashioned or rolled oats
⅓ cup almond milk
½ cup vanilla or plain Greek yogurt
⅛ cup blackberries
⅛ cup raspberries
⅛ cup blueberries

Strawberry, Chocolate, and Hazelnut Refrigerator Oats
Ingredients:
⅓ cup old-fashioned or rolled oats
⅓ cup milk of choice
½ cup Greek yogurt (strawberry or plain)
2 tbsp chocolate hazelnut spread
½ cup Greek yogurt
½ cup strawberries, chopped
pinch of salt
Topping: chopped hazelnuts

Apple Cinnamon Refrigerator Oats
Ingredients:
⅓ cup old-fashioned or rolled oats
⅓ cup milk
½ cup vanilla or plain Greek yogurt
½ cup apples, diced
1 tsp cinnamon
⅛ tsp nutmeg
Topping: crushed graham crackers

Pumpkin Pie Refrigerator Oats
Ingredients:
⅓ cup old-fashioned or rolled oats
⅓ cup vanilla almond milk
½ cup vanilla or plain Greek yogurt
¼ cup pumpkin puree
1 tsp pumpkin pie spice
      or
½ tsp cinnamon and ½ tsp nutmeg

Directions:

To assemble the overnight oats, place the ingredients in the jar in the same order as they're noted in the ingredient lists. Start with the oats, followed by the milk and then the yogurt. Add the fruit and/or spices and finish by adding the toppings called for in the recipe. Once the jars are full, refrigerate them overnight.

In the morning, take the jar out of the refrigerator and eat at home, or grab the jar and go so you can enjoy a delicious breakfast at work.

When you are ready to eat, enjoy the overnight oats cold directly from the jar.

Yogurt Parfaits

I'm a morning person. One of those rare creatures who loves getting their day started by being up bright and early. I get if from my mama; she's an early bird too. For those of you who don't like to greet the sun as it makes its grand entrance over the horizon, these parfaits are ideal. No hot water, no blender, just a delicious grab-and-go breakfast.

Jar: pint, wide mouth
Serves: 1

Basic Yogurt Parfait
Ingredients:
1 cup vanilla or plain yogurt
½ cup fruit of choice
¼ cup granola
1–2 tbsp toppings, optional

Peanut Butter Banana Yogurt Parfait
Ingredients:
1 cup vanilla yogurt
½ banana, sliced
2 tbsp peanut butter
¼ cup granola

Piña Colada Yogurt Parfait
Ingredients:
1 cup coconut yogurt
½ cup pineapple
¼ cup granola
1 tbsp toasted coconut flakes

Raspberry Lemonade Yogurt Parfait
Ingredients:
1 cup lemon yogurt
½ cup raspberries
1 tbsp lemon zest
¼ cup granola

Banana Cream Pie Yogurt Parfait
Ingredients:
1 cup vanilla yogurt
½ banana, sliced
¼ cup granola
2–3 vanilla wafers, crumbled

Directions:

To assemble the parfaits, place the ingredients in the jar in the same order as listed in each recipe, starting with the yogurt, and then adding the fruit. Next, add the granola and finish with the toppings if the recipe calls for them.

When you are ready to eat, enjoy the parfait directly from the jar.

Make-Ahead Smoothies

When I learned how to make all my smoothies ahead of time, I became a smoothie addict. Well, if I'm being completely honest, I became an even bigger smoothie addict. Add as much or as little greens as you'd like to these smoothies. Most mornings I like to load my smoothies up with spinach to give my body the vitamin K boost it needs.

Jar: quart, wide mouth
Serves: 1

Basic Smoothie
Ingredients:
2–4 cups frozen/fresh fruits and veggies
1 cup liquid (water, orange juice, coconut milk, coconut water, almond milk, milk, etc.)
¼ cup vanilla or plain yogurt, optional

Berry Me Smoothie
Ingredients:
1 cup frozen raspberries
1 cup frozen blueberries
½ cup frozen strawberries
¼ cup vanilla or plain Greek yogurt
1 cup vanilla almond milk

Green Machine Smoothie
Ingredients:
½ cucumber, diced
1 cup frozen pineapple
2 cups spinach, fresh or frozen
1 tsp lemon juice
1 cup water

Too Good to Be Green Smoothie
Ingredients:
1 cup fresh kale
1 cup fresh spinach
½ banana
½ cup frozen strawberries
½ cup blueberries
½ cup mango, chopped
1 cup water

Take Me Somewhere Tropical Smoothie
Ingredients:
½ cup frozen pineapple
½ banana
½ cup mango or peaches
1 cup strawberries
1 cup coconut milk

Directions:
Store frozen and fresh fruits and veggies in the mason jar. Seal the jars tightly with a lid. When you're ready to enjoy your smoothie, add your liquid of choice and yogurt, and then blend until smooth.

Smoothies can be enjoyed directly from the jar.

TIPS: I use a handheld immersion blender to eliminate the need for more dishwashing. The blender stick fits right inside the jar. If the jar is too full, the contents could end up all over your counter, so start slow and increase the speed as you go.

Mason jars can be frozen, but use caution when you do. Allow the jar to sit on the counter for two minutes or so to let the frozen fruit and veggies start to thaw a bit. This will make the smoothie blend faster.

If you choose to use fresh fruit and veggies, then you will need to add ice to make the mixture cold. Store these smoothies in the fridge. If you use a combination of fresh and frozen ingredients, then store the jar in the freezer.

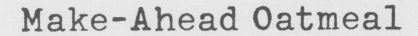

Make-Ahead Oatmeal

For those Mondays when you wake up still tired and you know you're going to need lots of energy to get you through those three meetings that are scheduled before lunch, or to survive teaching that kindergarten class. These grab-and-go oatmeal jars are customizable to suit your tastes. Make five on a Sunday night and be ready for the whole week.

Jar: pint, wide mouth
Serves: 1

Basic Oatmeal
Ingredients:
½ cup quick oats
1 tbsp brown sugar
½ cup dried or fresh fruit
1 cup hot water or milk
1–2 tbsp toppings or seasonings, optional

Apple Cinnamon Oatmeal
Ingredients:
½ cup quick oats
1 tbsp brown sugar
½ cup dried apples
⅛ tsp cinnamon
1 cup hot water or milk

Chocolate Banana Oatmeal
Ingredients:
½ cup quick oats
1 tbsp brown sugar
½ cup dried banana
2 tbsp dark chocolate chips
1 cup hot water or milk

Cherry Almond Oatmeal
Ingredients:
½ cup quick oats
1 tbsp brown sugar
¼ cup dried cherries
2 tbsp almonds
1 cup hot water or milk

Strawberry Banana Oatmeal
Ingredients:
½ cup quick oats
1 tbsp brown sugar
¼ cup dried banana
¼ cup dried strawberries
1 cup hot water or milk

Pineapple Coconut Oatmeal
Ingredients:
½ cup quick oats
1 tbsp brown sugar
½ cup dried pineapple
2 tbsp shredded coconut
1 cup hot water or milk

Directions:

To assemble the make-ahead oatmeal, place the ingredients in the jar in the same order as noted in the recipes, starting with the oats, then adding the sugar followed by the fruit. When you're ready to enjoy your oatmeal, carefully pour hot water or milk into the jar. Allow the jar to sit until the oats are cooked, approximately eight minutes. Handle with care, as the jar will be very hot.

TIPS: If you choose to use freeze-dried or dehydrated fruit, these oatmeal jars can be stored in the pantry. They have a shelf life of about six weeks. If you prefer fresh fruit, store them in the fridge.

Labeling the jars helps take the guesswork out of picking the perfect oatmeal for breakfast. A permanent marker works really well to write on the lid and washes off with soap and water.

Meals in a Jar

The task of creating meals in a jar was a little more challenging than creating salads. I turned to my coworkers, friends, and family for inspiration. One coworker in particular, a self-proclaimed mason jar expert, suggested recipes, brought in her mason jar lunches to show off, and helped me get the wheels turning for how I could make mason jars work for any meal of the day.

The idea of creating an entire meal in a jar without any special boxes or containers is very appealing to me, and hopefully to you as well. There are a few recipes for "deconstructed" meals in this section, including sushi and "sandwiches." There are also suggestions on how to pack a complete picnic lunch, from soup to nuts, so to speak. Once again, the mason jar becomes the ideal vessel for healthy, tasty food.

Breakfast Burrito in a Jar

I have made a few of these for breakfast in the past few months. They are so tasty and filling. I occasionally like to switch out the black beans for refried beans, add some green onions, or swap out the bacon for leftover steak. Mix things up and make it your own. Delicioso!

Jar: pint, wide mouth
Serves: 1

Ingredients:
1 tbsp olive oil or butter
1 corn tortilla, torn into pieces
2 eggs
⅛ tsp cumin
⅛ tsp paprika
2 tbsp cheese
¼ cup black beans
1 strip bacon, cooked and crumbled
1 tbsp salsa
¼ avocado, diced
sour cream, optional

Directions:
Put the oil in the jar. (If using butter, put it in the jar, then place in the microwave and cook for approximately 20 seconds to melt the butter.) Next, place half of the tortilla pieces into the bottom of the jar. In a small bowl, whisk together the eggs, cumin, and paprika. Pour the eggs into the jar on top of the tortilla, then top with the cheese.

Place the jar in the microwave and cook on high for 45–60 seconds. Using an oven mitt, carefully remove the jar from the microwave.

To assemble the burrito, add the remaining tortilla pieces to the jar, and then add the beans. Put in the crumbled bacon next, followed by the salsa. Top it all off with the diced avocado, and, if desired, add a dollop of sour cream.

Enjoy your breakfast burrito directly from the jar.

Microwave Quiche in a Jar

These breakfast jars can be made the evening before. Perfect for a holiday or a brunch get-together. Easy to prep and easy to serve, they can even be taken to work, uncooked, and microwaved for breakfast or lunch.

Jar: pint, wide mouth
Serves: 1

Ingredients:
1 tbsp butter
1 slice of bread, cubed
1–2 eggs, beaten
2 tbsp milk
¼ cup spinach, chopped
2–3 cherry tomatoes, halved
1 slice of ham or bacon, diced
1 tbsp cheddar cheese, shredded

Directions:
Put the butter into the jar, then place it in the microwave and cook on high for about 20 seconds, until the butter is melted. Next, add the bread cubes, eggs, and milk to the jar and stir until combined. Continue by adding the spinach and tomatoes, and then the ham or bacon. Lastly, add the cheddar. Stir to combine, and then press the ingredients down into the jar.

Put the jar into the microwave and cook on high for 1½–2 minutes, until set. Using an oven mitt, carefully remove the jar from the microwave.

Enjoy the quiche directly from the jar.

NOTE: Don't worry if the egg mixture starts to rise above the top of the jar in the microwave. It will settle back down once it stops cooking.

Chicken Parmesan "Sandwich"

Anyone else sing that "Chicken Parm you taste so good" jingle every time you see chicken parm on a restaurant menu? No, it's just me then? Well, you'll definitely be singing this recipe's praises after you try this "sandwich" in a jar.

Jar: quart
Serves: 1

Ingredients:
1 tbsp olive oil
1 small loaf ciabatta bread, cut into 1-inch cubes
2–3 tbsp tomato sauce
2 tbsp plain Greek yogurt
1 chicken breast, cooked and cubed
½ cup mozzarella ciliegine, halved
½ cup cherry tomatoes
shaved Parmesan, to taste

Directions:
Heat the oil in a skillet over medium heat then add the bread cubes, turning several times to toast all sides.

To assemble the "sandwich," first mix the tomato sauce and yogurt together in a bowl. Next, place half of the toasted bread cubes into the jar, followed by half of the chicken. Add ¼ cup mozzarella, 1½ tbsp of the tomato sauce-yogurt mixture, and ¼ cup of the tomatoes. Repeat, then top with the Parmesan.

When you are ready to eat, pour the contents into a bowl or enjoy directly from the jar.

TIP: This dish works well hot or cold. If you plan on heating the dish, either pour it into a bowl first, or use caution when heating it in the jar. For heating in a microwave, the recommended time is 1½–2 minutes.

Waldorf Chicken Salad "Sandwich"

The tart apples, juicy grapes, and creamy yogurt provide layers of flavors that will have you forgetting that this is a lightened up version of chicken salad layered in a mason jar!

Jars: pint, wide mouth
Serves: 2

Ingredients:
1 tbsp olive oil
1 small loaf ciabatta bread, cut into 1-inch cubes
½ cup plain Greek yogurt
2 tbsp lemon juice
1 tsp garlic powder
1 cup (3 oz) chicken breast, cooked and cubed
¼ cup red onion
⅓ cup green apple, diced
⅓ cup grapes, halved
¼ cup dried cranberries
¼ cup almonds

Directions:
Heat the oil in a skillet over medium heat then add the bread cubes, turning several times to toast all sides.

Allow the bread to cool while you mix together the chicken salad.

In a medium bowl, whisk together the yogurt, lemon juice, and garlic powder. To this mixture, add the chicken, onion, fruit, and almonds. Mix well to combine.

Alternate layers, putting half the bread cubes into the jar, then half the chicken salad. Add the remaining bread and top with the remaining chicken salad.

When you are ready to eat, pour the contents into a bowl or enjoy directly from the jar.

Picnic in a Jar

Tiny food is the best, isn't it? I am often on the hunt for miniature food for these picnic jars. Each jar is unique, based on what ingredients you have on hand or what you purchase at the store. I like to combine a little premade with a little homemade for my picnic in a jar. Below is one suggestion, pictured is another suggestion. Get creative with your miniature food.

Jar: quart
Serves: 1–2

Ingredients:
cookie
cracker
packaged cheese slice
salami, wrapped
pasta salad in a BNTO cup

Directions:
Place the ingredients into jars. Bring the self-contained picnic in a jar to your favorite spot and enjoy.

BBQ in a Jar

Who doesn't love a backyard BBQ? Well, now you can hold an entire BBQ in your hand! This layered lunch is great for using up leftover food, or create a batch to have for lunch during the week.

Jar: quart
Serves: 1

Ingredients:
½ cup baked beans
½ cup corn
1 cup barbecue pork, shredded
1–2 tbsp barbecue sauce
½ cup coleslaw
2 tbsp cheddar cheese, shredded
2 tbsp green onion, chopped

Directions:
To get this BBQ in a jar started, pour the baked beans into the jar. Next up, add the corn followed by the shredded pork. Top the pork with the barbecue sauce, and then layer in the coleslaw. Top with shredded cheddar and green onions.

When you are ready to eat, pour the contents into a bowl or enjoy directly from the jar.

Taco Bar Picnic

This taco bar falls right in line with my "everything you'll need in one container" fascination I mentioned in the introduction. There are so many ways to put a mason jar taco bar together, and this is just one suggestion. Use what you have on hand, make it vegetarian with roasted veggies instead of meat, or change the direction altogether and make gyros with pita, lamb, feta, and onions, all served up in mason jars.

Jars: various
Serves: many

Ingredients:
beans
cheese
meat
shredded lettuce
corn tortillas
salsa
crema
spicy pickled vegetables

Directions:
Put each ingredient in a separate jar. Pack the jars in a cooler or picnic basket with an ice pack. Once you arrive at your picnic location, set up the taco salad bar for your own fiesta.

Deconstructed Sushi

For all those sushi fans out there, now you can have sushi in a jar! All the traditional sushi ingredients are layered in a mason jar for a great make-ahead lunch. Once again, use your imagination. Use your favorite sushi roll as the inspiration for your own deconstructed sushi.

Jar: pint
Serves: 1

Ingredients:
1 sheet nori (seaweed paper) or roasted seaweed sheets
½ cup sticky rice
¼ cup cucumber, julienned
¼ cup carrot, shredded
½ avocado, diced
pickled ginger, to taste
wasabi, to taste, optional

Directions:
To construct the deconstructed sushi, you'll layer the ingredients in the jar, starting with ½ sheet nori. Next, add ¼ cup rice, followed by the cucumber and carrot. Put in the remaining rice and the other half of the sheet of nori, then top with the avocado. Finally toss in the desired amount of pickled ginger If you're feeling brave, add the wasabi when you are ready to eat.

You can pour the contents into a bowl or eat it directly from the jar.

Instant Noodles in a Jar

Now you can enjoy the flavor and ease of an instant cup of noodles without all the sodium. This fully customizable noodle dish is perfect for a chilly afternoon. Test out different flavor combinations to see which ones are to your liking.

Jar: pint
Serves: 1

Ingredients:

1–3 tsp Flavor Base
Chicken, beef, or vegetable stock
   concentrate*
miso paste or curry paste

1–3 tsp Flavor Boost
sesame oil
soy sauce
rice wine vinegar
dried seasons/herbs
chili-garlic sauce
hot sauce
garlic/ginger paste
citrus zest

½ cup Chopped Veggies/Protein
cooked meat
corn
carrots
edamame
peas
tofu
mushrooms
spinach
zucchini

1 cup Noodles**
udon
ramen
soba
spaghetti
rice noodles
dry rice noodle
sticks
vermicelli noodles

Fresh Ingredients, to taste
fresh herbs
green onions
bean sprouts
lime

* Better Than Bouillon brand is recommended.

** Cook noodles 1 minute less than package directions. Rinse with cold water to stop the noodles from cooking further. Drain and toss in olive oil to prevent the noodles from sticking together.

Directions:

To assemble the soup, choose one or more from each section of the ingredients list and place them in the jar in the following order: flavor base, flavor boost, veggies/protein, noodles, fresh ingredients. Once all of the ingredients are in the jar, seal the jar and store it in the refrigerator.

When you are ready to eat, remove the top and fill the jar with just enough boiling water to cover the noodles. Return the lid to the jar. Allow it to steep for 2–3 minutes. Then, gently stir the ingredients with a fork or chopsticks, ensuring that you reach the flavor base on the bottom. The contents and jar will be very hot, so use caution. Enjoy immediately.

Creamy Polenta

This polenta recipe is very creamy and allows you to show your creativity in how you choose to top it. My favorite combinations are ricotta and green onions and steak and cheddar. But, honestly, I could eat polenta for breakfast, lunch, and dinner with almost anything on top. For a lighter version, substitute 2 cups of chicken broth or water for the milk and half & half.

Jars: pint, wide mouth
Serves: 3

Ingredients:
2 cups milk
1¼ cups half & half
¾ cup instant polenta
1 tbsp unsalted butter
¼ cup Parmesan cheese, shaved
salt and pepper, to taste

Directions:
In a large saucepan, bring the milk and half & half to a rolling boil over medium heat. Reduce the heat to low and add the polenta. Whisking constantly, cook for 5–7 minutes, until the mixture has thickened. If the mixture seems too thick, add more milk to thin the polenta out.

When the consistency is that of thick oatmeal, whisk in the butter and Parmesan cheese, then season with salt and pepper, to taste.

Split the polenta between the three jars then add your favorite toppings.

When it's ready, enjoy the polenta directly from the jar.

Topping suggestions:
- sautéed mushrooms and thyme
- sausage and tomato sauce
- steak and cheddar cheese
- roasted vegetables
- sautéed tomatoes and spinach
- pesto and pine nuts
- ricotta and green onions
- shrimp and peppers
- chili
- corn and cotija cheese
- bacon and eggs
- asparagus and crispy prosciutto
- shredded BBQ pork and grilled onions

Desserts

While the idea of desserts in a healthy cookbook seems counterproductive, I'm a firm believer in treating yourself every once in a while. These dessert jars are perfectly portioned to be just enough of a treat to satisfy your sweet tooth, but not so much that you sacrifice your healthy eating habits.

Although I'm more of a salty snacks person, I found myself excited to create, test, and taste these tiny treats. All of the recipes are easy to make and use ingredients that keep them as light as possible. Made in a small batch for a party or just for one, these dessert jars are great to enjoy after dinner . . . or maybe even as a before-dinner snack.

Banana Split Trifle

This trifle recipe is a lightened up version of a traditional banana split, giving you all the best parts of a banana split, but without all the pesky calories you get from the ice cream. Made with vanilla yogurt, you can make these tasty treats the night before for an easy dessert or even a sweet breakfast.

Jar: pint
Serves: 1

Ingredients:
1 cup vanilla yogurt
1 banana, sliced
½ cup strawberries, diced
3 tbsp pineapple preserves
chocolate sauce, to drizzle
whipped topping, optional
1 maraschino cherry

Directions:
To create this tasty trifle, start by placing ½ cup of the yogurt into your jar. Next, add about half of the banana slices and half of the strawberries. Place the pineapple preserves in the jar, followed by the remaining yogurt. Repeat the layers of fruit as before, then drizzle on the chocolate sauce. If desired, add the whipped topping and garnish with the cherry.

This dish is best when eaten directly from the jar.

Sweet Strawberry Peach Panzanella

This recipe is one of my favorites, and for it to be a dessert, that's saying something. I first had strawberries and balsamic vinegar together when I was in college at a fancy dinner party thrown by a very talented chef friend of mine. It was served on top of good vanilla ice cream, and I remember thinking that it was an odd pairing for dessert. Man, was I wrong. Now I think the combination of strawberries and balsamic with the addition of creamy goat cheese is perfection.

Jar: pint
Serves: 1

Ingredients:
2 tbsp balsamic vinegar or balsamic vinegar syrup
½ cup strawberries, diced
½ peach, diced
2 tbsp goat cheese
2 basil leaves, chiffonade
1 cup pound cake, cubed

Directions:
To create this easy dessert panzanella, start with the balsamic vinegar on the bottom of the jar followed by the strawberries, and then the diced peach. Toss in the goat cheese and basil. Finally, drop in the cubes of pound cake.

When it's time for dessert, pour the contents of the jar into a bowl and enjoy.

No-Bake Key Lime Cheesecake

I have very talented cheesecake–making family and friends. Three different types of cheesecakes grace my table for three different occasions. My friend's mom makes a creamy birthday cheesecake that I adore. My best friend's dad makes pumpkin cheesecake for Thanksgiving, which is divine. And my Auntie Jill makes the most amazing homemade cheesecake with strawberries for Christmas. Considering the fight over these adorable little jars, this key lime cheesecake may become my trademark cheesecake.

Jars: half-pint
Serves: 4

Ingredients:
Crust
1 cup graham cracker crumbs (approx. 4–6 crackers)
2–3 tbsp granulated sugar
pinch of salt
3 tbsp unsalted butter, melted

Filling
1 8-oz package of cream cheese, softened
½ can (7-oz) sweetened condensed milk
½ cup freshly squeezed key lime juice (bottled works as well)
2 key limes, zested
½ cup whipped topping

Directions:
Place the graham cracker crumbs, sugar, and salt into a medium bowl and stir with a fork until well combined. Drizzle the melted butter into the crumb and sugar mixture and stir to combine. Evenly distribute the graham cracker mixture between four half-pint jars. Press slightly.

In a large bowl, mix the cream cheese, condensed milk, lime juice, and lime zest together until smooth. Gently fold in the whipped topping. Spoon or pipe this mixture into the jars on top of the graham cracker crusts. Refrigerate at least 5 hours or until firm.

TIP: For easy filling, I like to put a large resealable plastic bag into a cup or quart mason jar and fold the opening over the edges of the jar. I spoon the cream cheese filling into the bag, then press the mixture to one corner. Snip off a corner of the bag to create a small hole. Then I pipe the mixture into the jars.

Blackberry Crisp

With just a few simple ingredients, many of which might already be in your kitchen, you can create a delicious dessert that's perfect for a picnic by the beach. If you want, you can top this dessert off with a big scoop of ice cream; go ahead, you know you want to.

Jars: half pint
Serves: 6

Ingredients:
Filling
4 cups blackberries, rinsed
⅓ cup granulated sugar
2 tbsp cornstarch

Topping
½ cup all-purpose flour
¼ cup granulated sugar
½ cup brown sugar
¼ tsp salt
½ cup old-fashioned oats
4 tbsp butter, chilled
¼ tsp cinnamon

Directions:
Preheat the oven to 350°F.

Put the ingredients for the filling into a large saucepan over medium heat. Using a potato masher or fork, slightly mash the blackberries as they cook. Stir the mixture as it cooks to keep the sugars from burning. Cook until the mixture has thickened, approximately 8–10 minutes. Remove the pan from the heat and set aside to cool.

Place all of the ingredients for the topping into a bowl and combine with a fork or your hands until the mixture is crumbly.

Fill the jars halfway with the blackberry mixture. Divide the topping among the six jars, about ¼ cup per jar, on top of the blackberries. Place the jars in a 6-cup muffin pan and bake for 20–25 minutes or until the mixture is bubbly and the crumb topping is golden brown. Carefully remove the tray from the oven. The jars will be very hot. Allow them to cool before serving or storing in the refrigerator.

NOTE: I'm excited to have brought a bit of my muffin pan past into this recipe; a little muffin pan meets mason jar—a match made in heaven.

Salted Caramel Apple Pie Trifle

Delicious and sweet apple pie in the convenience of a mason jar. The addition of salted caramel is up to you, but I ask, why not salted caramel?

Jars: pint
Serves: 2

Ingredients:
2 apples, diced
2 tsp brown sugar
2 tbsp butter
1 tsp cinnamon
6–7 oatmeal cookies, crumbled
2 scoops of ice cream or whipped topping
caramel, for drizzling
salt, to taste

Directions:
In a saucepan over low heat, cook the apples, brown sugar, butter, and cinnamon until the apples are soft, approximately 10–15 minutes. Allow the apples to cool before adding them to the jar.

To create this tasty trifle, fill the jar by alternating layers of the apple mixture with layers of the oatmeal cookie crumbles. Top with ice cream or whipped topping then drizzle the caramel on top followed by a pinch of salt.

TIP: If you plan to take this with you on a picnic or to work, leave out the ice cream or whipped topping. Instead, you can add vanilla yogurt. But keep the salted caramel . . . always keep the caramel.

"Bring the Bubbles" Cocktails

I almost didn't write this section. I had a hard time deciding if a book with nutritious salads and healthy snacks really needed a chapter dedicated to drinking. I tossed the idea back and forth with my friends to see how they felt about this "unheathly" detour. The general consensus from this always honest bunch was: "Why not, Amy?" If it makes me happy, I should go forth and mix that cocktail, my friends said. And so I did.

Harnessing my love for camping and picnics, I created these "Bring the Bubbles" drink recipes, perfect for a crowd or for a party of one. Each recipe calls for bubbles of some kind.

Whether it's the end of a long day, or the end of the cookbook writing process, sometimes you just need to settle down in your easy chair with a mason jar michelada and say, "I earned this."

White Wine Camper Sangria

When I go camping, which I really enjoy doing, I always make sure to pack the essentials: tent, sleeping bag, cast-iron pan, and Camper Sangria. Packed in the cooler next to the bacon and eggs, this fancy sangria will make sleeping on the ground seem a little less like camping and a little more like glamping. The fruits in this recipe can be changed out based on the season. Grapes and strawberries also work really well.

Jars: pint
Servings: 4

Ingredients:
8 tbsp peach nectar or purée
1 cup fresh berries
2 large peaches, diced
1 bottle dry white wine (sauvignon blanc is a good option)
4 oz vodka (peach flavored works well)
club soda

Directions:
Start filling each of the four jars with 2 tbsp of the peach purée, and then divide the fruit evenly among the jars. Next, add 1 oz of vodka and approximately 1¼ cups of white wine to each jar.

Place the jars in the cooler overnight. (For those of you who are glamping or go "camping" in your backyard, place the jars in the refrigerator overnight.) When ready to serve, fill the jar the rest of the way with the club soda and enjoy responsibly.

Red Wine Camper Sangria

Just in case you're not a white wine person and are more of a traditionalist when it comes to sangria, I've included this Red Wine Camper Sangria for you. This recipe has all the traditional aspects of Spanish sangria with the sweet addition of lemon-lime soda. The mason jar pictured here is a half gallon jar.

Jars: pint
Serves: 6

Ingredients:
1 granny smith apple, sliced
1 orange, sliced
1 lemon, sliced
1 botttle dry red wine (cabernet sauvignon is a good option)
½ cup brandy
lemon-lime soda

Directions:
Start by dividing the fruit among the six jars. In a pitcher or large mason jar, mix the red wine and brandy together. Divide the brandy and wine mixture among the six jars. Place the jars in the cooler overnight. (For those of you who are glamping or go "camping" in your backyard, place the jars in the refrigerator overnight.) When ready to serve, fill the jars the rest of the way with the soda and enjoy responsibly.

Mason Jar Mojito

When I was a senior in high school, my family and I had the incredible honor of traveling to Cuba to help deliver medical supplies. It was one of the most amazing experiences of my life. The cars, the music, the people, the food, everything was enchanting. One night my parents gave in and let me have a mojito. No mojito since has compared to it. This mason jar mojito is a humble homage to that perfect mojito.

Jar: pint
Serves: 1

Ingredients:
6–8 fresh mint leaves
juice of one lime, plus one wedge for garnish
1 tbsp sugar/simple syrup
enough ice to fill the jar
1.5 oz white rum
club soda

Directions:
Place the mint leaves, lime juice, and sugar into the jar. Using a muddler or the end of a wooden spoon, muddle, or mash, the mint and lime juice into the sugar. This breaks down the mint, bringing out the oils from the leaves. The mixture may require more lime, sugar, or mint, depending on your taste. Taste it and add additional mint, lime juice, or sugar if desired.

Once the mixture tastes just right to you, fill the jar with ice. Next, pour in the rum, then add club soda until the jar is full.

Pimm's Cup

. . . .

I had a lot of fun with this recipe. I learned about the history of Pimm's No. 1, created in the nineteenth century, and its recipe, which only a handful of people were privy to. I really enjoyed this coctkail and all its garnishes. With the addition of ginger beer this drink is full of flavor and great for a party.

Jar: pint
Serves: 1

Ingredients:
1 slice of lemon
1–3 cucumber slices
1.5 oz Pimm's No. 1
cherry, to garnish
enough ice to fill the jar
1 bottle of ginger beer

Directions:
Place the lemon and cucumber slices in the jar first. Next, pour in a shot of Pimm's No. 1. When you are ready to serve, add the ice, and then pour in enough ginger beer to fill the jar. Garnish with a cherry.

Michelada

This is my go-to drink for . . . well, any time of day really. This recipe varies from country to country. I like my michelada spicy, with lots of lime and a salted rim. Feel free to experiment to find what suits your taste.

Jar: quart
Serves: 1

Ingredients:
salt for the glass
1 tsp celery salt
2 lime wedges
4 oz. tomato juice
2 dashes Worcestershire sauce
4 dashes Tabasco or preferred hot sauce
juice from 1½ limes
enough ice to fill the jar
1 bottle Mexican beer (I prefer Dos Equis Amber)

Directions:
If you plan on salting the rim of the jar, combine the salt and celery salt together. Use one of the lime wedges to coat the rim of the jar, then dip the top of the jar into the salt mixture.

Next, pour the tomato juice into the jar then add the Worcestershire sauce, Tabasco, and lime juice. Put a lid on the jar and keep it sealed until ready to serve.

When it's that time of day for you, add ice and then enough beer to fill the jar.

Whiskey Jam Cocktail

A lightbulb went off when I created this recipe. I'm surprised that I didn't think of adding jam to my cocktails before. It adds the perfect amount of sweetness and flavoring to this sparkling drink. My dad is a big fan of peanut butter and jelly sandwiches, so there is a steady collection of jams, jellies, and preserves in my parents' fridge. I experimented around with different flavors of preserves until I came up with the aromatic and slightly sweet combination of blackberry and thyme.

Jar: pint
Serves: 1

Ingredients:
1.5 oz bourbon whiskey of your choice
1 tbsp blackberry preserves
1 sprig thyme
enough ice to fill the jar
1 can lime-flavored sparkling water, such as Perrier or Pellegrino

Directions:
Put the whiskey, preserves, and thyme into the jar. Close the lid and shake to combine. This helps break down the preserves and flavors the whiskey. Keep the jar closed until ready to serve.

When it's cocktail time, add the ice, then add enough sparkling water to fill the jar.

Snacks in a Jar

The beauty of this section is the flexibility to create food for one or for a crowd. The dips, for example, make a great addition to any barbecue, and the roasted chickpeas can be a lifesaver on long car rides. While sharing is always encouraged, you have my permission to keep these recipes all to yourself. The midday snack attack is a very real thing for me.

While the mason jar salads and mason jar meals are designed to be filling, there may still come a point in your day when all you need is some ranch hummus and veggies to get yourself operating at one hundred percent again. I like to keep a whole jar of one recipe in my work fridge and portion myself out whatever I feel I need. This can take significant restraint, however, so portion-size jars work well.

Another bonus of these snack jars is that they cut down on waste. Like all the other recipes, once you're finished eating, the jars are easily washed and reused. Just add eco-friendly to the mason jar's long list of fine qualities.

Roasted Garlic Parmesan Chickpeas

My family LOVES popcorn, but traditional popcorn has been pushed aside to make way for the new "popcorn" in our house. These Roasted Garlic Parmesan Chickpeas offer the crunch and slightly salty snack that my family craves, but without the extra salt we're trying to cut out of our diet.

Jar: pint
Serves: 1

Ingredients:
1 15-oz can chickpeas
1½ tbsp olive oil
1 tsp garlic powder
½ tsp oregano
2 tbsp Parmesan, finely grated
salt, to taste

Directions:
Preheat the oven to 400°F.

Drain and rinse the chickpeas, then dry them between layers of paper towels and allow at least 10 minutes for the excess moisture to be soaked up.

While the chickpeas are drying, mix the olive oil, garlic powder, oregano, and Parmesan together in a bowl. Taste and add salt if desired.

Once the chickpeas are dry, add them to the bowl and mix until they are well coated in the garlic–parmesan mixture. Once they are sufficiently coated, transfer the chickpeas to a baking sheet.

Bake in the preheated oven for 30 minutes. Halfway through roasting, give the pan a shake to loosen the chickpeas. Once they're done cooking, remove the pan from the oven and allow the chickpeas to cool completely. Once cooled, store the "popcorn" in an airtight jar.

NOTE: The Roasted Garlic Parmesan Chickpeas will last two to three days in an airtight container.

Ranch Hummus with Veggies

Ranch is a complex, recognizable flavor. This hummus doesn't use oil, so it is on the healthier side of snacks. This would be the perfect snack to bring to work for a midday energy boost.

Jar: 1½ pint or quart, wide mouth, and BNTO cup
Yields: 2 cups

Ingredients:
1 can chickpeas
2 tbsp tahini
⅓ cup plain Greek yogurt
1 tsp dried dill
½ tsp onion powder
½ tsp garlic salt
1 tsp dried parsley
1 tbsp lemon juice
1 cup veggies of your choice, cut into sticks

Directions:
Drain the can of chickpeas, reserving the liquid.

Combine the chickpeas, tahini, yogurt, dill, onion powder, garlic salt, parsley, and lemon juice or ranch seasoning mix in a blender or food processor. Pulse until smooth. If the mixture is too thick, gradually add the reserved chickpea liquid until it has reach the desired consistency.

Fill the BNTO cup with ½ cup of the ranch hummus. Place the veggie sticks into a 1½ pint or quart mason jar. Place the BNTO cup into the top of the jar and close the lid.

TIP: To simplify making the hummus, just substitute 1½ tbsp of ranch seasoning mix for the dry seasonings.

Bruschetta and Baguette Chips

This classic Italian dish combines simple, fresh ingredients for a very tasty appetizer. Bruschetta and baguette chips beg to be eaten by the mason jarful.

Jar: Various
Yields: 2 cups

Ingredients:
4–5 tomatoes, diced
1 clove garlic, minced
4–5 basil leaves, chiffonade
2 tbsp olive oil
salt and pepper, to taste
1 cup baguette chips

Directions:
In a medium bowl, combine the tomatoes, garlic, basil, olive oil, and salt and pepper. Let the mixture sit in the refrigerator for at least 30 minutes before serving.

Put at least 1 cup of the bruschetta into a mason jar. Place the baguette chips (or toasted bread slices if you prefer) into a BNTO cup. Place the BNTO cup into the top of the mason jar, then close the lid.

Strawberry Jalapeño Salsa with Cinnamon Sugar Pita Chips

I think the best part of this recipe is how beautiful the colors are. The dark pink strawberries, the soft purple of the onions, the vibrant green of the cilantro, and the deep green of the jalapeño.

Jar: various
Yields: 2 cups

Ingredients:
2 cups strawberries, diced
¼ cup red onion, diced
½–1 jalapeño, finely diced
2 tbsp cilantro, chopped
2 tbsp lime juice (juice of one lime)
salt and pepper, to taste
1 cup cinnamon sugar pita chips

Directions:
In a medium bowl, combine the strawberries, onion, jalapeño, cilantro, and lime juice. If desired, add salt and pepper.

Pack the cinnamon sugar pita chips into a mason jar. Fill a BNTO cup with ½ cup of the salsa. Place the cup inside the top of the mason jar, then close the lid.

NOTE: This sweet and spicy snack should be served immediately or stored in the refrigerator for no more than 24 hours.

Garlic Lemon Feta Dip with Pretzel Chips

Oh my goodness, this dip is to die for. I love the combination of lemon and dill. There is so much delicious garlic and salty feta that I know it will be hard for you to not eat this all in one sitting. But, I encourage you to try.

Jar: various
Yields: 2 cups

Ingredients:
8 oz cream cheese, softened
6 oz feta, crumbled
4 garlic cloves, peeled
1 small shallot, chopped
2 tbsp lemon juice
1 tbsp dill
3 tbsp olive oil
salt and pepper, to taste
1 cup pretzel chips

Directions:
Combine the cream cheese and feta in a food processor. Pulse until thoroughly combined. Add the garlic, shallot, lemon juice, dill, and olive oil. If desired, add salt and pepper. Pulse until smooth, approximately 2–3 minutes.

Pack the pretzel chips into a mason jar. Fill a BNTO cup with ½ cup of the dip. Place the BNTO cup into the top of the mason jar, and then close the lid.

TIP: Not interested in going through the whole tedious ordeal of peeling garlic? Try this handy mason jar garlic peeling tip! Place a head of garlic inside a quart- or pint-size mason jar. Screw the lid on tightly and shake, shake, shake! As the garlic bounces around, it begins to peel itself. Pour the contents out onto a plate or cutting board and pick out the whole cloves of garlic. If some remain unpeeled, put them back in the jar and give them a few more shakes until they are all peeled. And voila, you have your peeled garlic!

Layered Dip with Tortilla Chips

This layered dip is great for setting out at a party or to have on hand for packed lunches.

Jars: half pint
Serves: 6

Ingredients:
1 (16-oz) can refried beans
1 (8-oz) container guacamole
1 (8-oz) container sour cream
1 (12-oz) container salsa
1 cup shredded Mexican blend cheese
4 green onions, sliced
1 cup tortilla chips per serving

Directions:
To assemble each dip jar, layer approximately 2 tablespoons of each ingredient in the same order as listed above, starting with the refried beans and topping the jar with the green onions.

Serve with the tortilla chips stored in a separate container.

Dressings

Most of the salads in this cookbook are accompanied by a basic vinaigrette dressing. I prefer vinaigrettes to creamier dressings when creating the bulk of my own personal salads. I have a cabinet full of different types of vinegars and oils to use when making my vinaigrettes.

A vinaigrette has two basic parts, oil and vinegar, and then different spices and seasonings are added depending on the taste desired.

When choosing oils and vinegars, I like to use high-quality ingredients; a good olive oil can make all the difference.

Many of these recipes call for you to shake to combine, though you can also whisk the ingredients together for a more thoroughly combined and thicker vinaigrette.

Balsamic Vinaigrette

Ingredients:
3 tbsp olive oil
1 tbsp balsamic vinegar
1 tsp honey
pinch of salt
pepper, to taste

Directions:
Put all of the ingredients into a small mason jar. Close the lid tightly and shake vigorously to combine. Dressing will separate if not used immediately.

(Spicy Cilantro) Lime Vinaigrette

Ingredients:
3 tbsp olive oil
2 tbsp lime juice
pinch of salt
1 tsp jalapeños, diced, optional
1 tbsp cilantro, chopped, optional

Directions:
Put all of the ingredients into a blender. Pulse until the ingredients are thoroughly combined. Pour the dressing into a small mason jar.

Honey-Lime Poppy Seed Dressing

Ingredients:
2 tbsp lime juice
3 tbsp olive oil
1 tsp honey
1 tsp Dijon mustard
¼ tbsp poppy seeds

Directions:
Put all of the ingredients into a small mason jar. Close the lid tightly and shake to combine.

White Wine Vinaigrette

Ingredients:
3 tbsp olive oil
2 tbsp white wine vinegar
pinch of salt
pepper, to taste

Directions:
Put all of the ingredients into a small mason jar. Close the lid tightly and shake to combine.

Garlic Lemon Dijon Vinaigrette

Ingredients:
3 tbsp olive oil
2 tbsp white wine vinegar
½ tbsp garlic, grated
1 tbsp lemon juice
¼ tsp dried thyme
¼ tsp salt
¼ tsp pepper
1 tsp Dijon mustard
1 tbsp honey

Directions:
Put all of the ingredients into a small mason jar. Close the lid tightly and shake to combine.

Citrus Ginger Vinaigrette

Ingredients:

3 tbsp grape-seed oil
2 tbsp rice wine vinegar
1 tbsp orange juice
1 tsp ginger paste
½ tsp sesame seeds
½ tsp honey
pinch of salt

Directions:

Put all of the ingredients into a small mason jar. Close the lid tightly and shake to combine.

Lemon Vinaigrette

Ingredients:

3 tbsp olive oil
2 tbsp lemon juice
pinch of salt
fresh ground pepper, to taste

Directions:

Put all of the ingredients into a small mason jar. Close the lid tightly and shake to combine.

Red Wine Vinaigrette

Ingredients:

3 tbsp olive oil
2 tbsp red wine vinegar
pinch of salt
pepper, to taste
½ tbsp shallots, minced, optional

Directions:

Put all of the ingredients into a small mason jar. Close the lid tightly and shake to combine.

Apple Cider Vinaigrette

Ingredients:

3 tbsp olive oil
2 tbsp apple cider vinegar
½ tsp honey
pinch of salt
pepper, to taste

Directions:

Put all of the ingredients into a small mason jar. Close the lid tightly and shake to combine.

White Balsamic Vinaigrette

Ingredients:

3 tbsp olive oil
1 tbsp white balsamic vinegar
½ tsp honey
pinch of salt
pepper, to taste

Directions:

Put all of the ingredients into a small mason jar. Close the lid tightly and shake vigorously to combine. Dressing will separate if not used immediately.

(Curry) Tahini Vinaigrette

Ingredients:

3 tbsp olive oil
1 tbsp white wine vinegar
1 tbsp tahini
1 tsp lemon juice
pinch of salt
pepper, to taste
½–1 tsp curry powder, optional

Directions:

Put all of the ingredients into a small mason jar. Close the lid tightly and shake to combine.

(Chipotle) Creamy Avocado Dressing

Ingredients:

3 tbsp plain Greek yogurt
3 tbsp olive oil
¼ ripe avocado
2 tbsp lemon juice
1 tbsp water
1 tbsp cilantro, chopped
½–1 tsp chipotle powder, optional

Directions:

Put all of the ingredients into a blender. Pulse until the ingredients are fully combined. Pour into a small mason jar.

Creamy BBQ Ranch Dressing

Ingredients:

2 tbsp Greek yogurt
½ tsp honey
1 tsp lemon juice
1 tbsp barbecue sauce
1 tsp ranch dressing or ½ tsp ranch dip
   seasoning mix

Directions:

Whisk all ingredients together in a bowl until fully combined, then transfer to a small mason jar.

Spicy Peanut Dressing

Ingredients:

2 tbsp smooth peanut butter
1 tbsp olive oil
1 tsp sesame oil
1 tbsp rice wine vinegar
1–2 tsp sriracha, to taste
1 tsp soy sauce
1 tsp brown sugar
1 tsp garlic, minced
¼ tsp ginger paste

Directions:

Whisk all ingredients together in a bowl until fully combined, then transfer to a small mason jar.

Honey Lime Dressing

Ingredients:

3 tbsp plain Greek yogurt
1 tbsp honey
1 tbsp lime juice
½ tsp lime zest

Directions:

Whisk all ingredients together in a bowl until fully combined, then transfer to a small mason jar.

Creamy Pesto Dressing

Ingredients:

2 tbsp pesto
3 tbsp plain Greek yogurt
1 tbsp white wine vinegar

Directions:

Whisk all ingredients together in a bowl until fully combined, then transfer to a small mason jar.

In Gratitude

I wouldn't feel right submitting this book without saying thank you to all the people who have helped me through this creative process. Though I've been here before, I needed even more love and support this time around to complete this cookbook.

I have to start with the biggest thank-you of all. Thank you Mom and Dad for supporting me in every way possible, not just during this book-writing process, but every day of my life. Thank you for the trips to the grocery store, cleaning up after me when I pulled all-nighters, and for generally letting me freak out while you took care of the little things. I will repay the favor tenfold when I am rich and famous one day. Until then, all I can say is THANK YOU, THANK YOU, THANK YOU! from the bottom of my heart!

Thank you to my oh-so-talented brother and sister for keeping things light when the struggle is real. Joe, congrats on the very impressive firefighting gig in San Francisco. I am beyond proud. And Becky, you are so talented and brave. You don't let anything stop you from doing what you love. We could all learn a little bit about following our hearts from you.

To my friends who, through the course of writing this book, have had to pick me up off the floor and push me forward, I can't thank you enough. Nadia, Robert, Fiona, Ram, Deanna, Caitlin, Lisa A., Lisa B., Kanoa, Kimi, Emily, Greggy, and Shannon—thank you for lending an ear, a spare room, a kitchen, a distraction, an open heart, and the occasional beer. Life takes you places you don't expect, but turns out it's exactly where you ought to be. I appreciate you being right there to welcome me back home. Thanks to your love and support, I am "Thirty, flirty, and thriving!"

To Beck, for your expert photography advice, thank you for answering all of my questions, big or small, and for taking those gorgeous photos for me. I am so grateful to have such a talented friend. And thank you to Kate for ALL the photography equipment, without which the photography process wouldn't have gone so smoothly.

As always, to my HA HA family, thank you for EVERYTHING. You are so supportive of all my endeavors. You cook for me when I'm hungry, you make me laugh when I need it most, and take me to Disneyland when all else fails. Some people search their whole lives for what we have; I'm so lucky to have already found my people. Ha Ha.

To those I have not mentioned by name but have thanked in person, my gratitude for you knows no bounds. I am so blessed to have family and friends in my life who encourage me, take care of me, and, most importantly, who love me unconditionally. I love you all so much!

Thank you to Brooke Rockwell for helping me say what I had trouble putting into words. I appreciate your patience and creativity. And last but not least, thank you to the staff at Skyhorse Publishing for having faith in me once again. I hope I made you proud.

Fahrenheit	Celcius	Gas Mark
225°	110°	¼
250°	120°	½
275°	140°	1
300°	150°	2
325°	160°	3
350°	180°	4
375°	190°	5
400°	200°	6
425°	220°	7
450°	230°	8

METRIC AND IMPERIAL CONVERSIONS
(These conversions are rounded for convenience)

Ingredient	Cups/Tablespoons/Teaspoons	Ounces	Grams/Milliliters
Oil	1 cup=16 tablespoons	7.5 ounces	209 grams
Cheese, shredded	1 cup	4 ounces	110 grams
Flour, all-purpose	1 cup/1 tablespoon	4.5 ounces/0.3 ounces	125 grams/8 grams
Fruit, dried	1 cup	4 ounces	120 grams
Fruits or veggies, chopped	1 cup	5 to 7 ounces	145 to 200 grams
Fruits or veggies, puréed	1 cup	8.5 ounces	245 grams
Honey or maple syrup	1 tablespoon	.75 ounces	20 grams
Liquids: milks, water, vinegar, or juice	1 cup	8 fluid ounces	240 milliliters
Salt	1 teaspoon	0.2 ounces	6 grams
Spices: cinnamon, cloves, ginger, or nutmeg (ground)	1 teaspoon	0.2 ounces	5 milliliters

Index

5 B Salad, 43

A

Almonds
  Broccoli, Almond, and Cherry Salad, 61
  Candied Nuts, xxi
  Cherry Almond Oatmeal, 98
  Chinese Chicken Salad, 37
  Cranberry and Brussels Sprouts Salad, 15
  Waldorf Chicken Salad "Sandwich," 109
  Watermelon, Feta, and Arugula Salad, 19
Antipasto Salad with Mixed Greens, 51
Apple Cider Vinaigrette, 165
  Honeycrisp and Spinach Salad, 47
Apple cider vinegar
  Apple Cider Vinaigrette, 165
Apple Cinnamon Oatmeal, 98
Apple Cinnamon Refrigerator Oats, 86
Apples
  Apple Cinnamon Oatmeal, 98
  Apple Cinnamon Refrigerator Oats, 86
  Honeycrisp and Spinach Salad, 47
  Red Wine Camper Sangria, 139
  Salted Caramel Apple Pie Trifle, 133
Waldorf Chicken Salad "Sandwich," 109
Artichokes
  Antipasto Salad with Mixed Greens, 51
  Mediterranean Artichoke and Spinach Salad, 55
Arugula
  Arugula, Pear, and Gorgonzola Salad, 11
  Asian Pear and Cashew Salad, 25
  Mango, Strawberry, and Arugula Salad, 27
  Prosciutto, Melon, and Arugula Salad, 41
  Watermelon, Feta, and Arugula Salad, 19
Arugula, Pear, and Gorgonzola Salad, 11
Asian Pear and Cashew Salad, 25
Avocado and White Bean Salad, 73
Avocados
  Avocado and White Bean Salad, 73
  Breakfast Burrito in a Jar, 103

Chickpea, Avocado, and Kale Salad, 17
Chipotle Creamy Avocado Dressing, 166
Chipotle Sweet Potato, Black Bean, and Kale Salad, 45
Deconstructed Sushi, 117
Guacamole Salad, 9
Mango, Strawberry, and Arugula Salad, 27
Mexican Avocado Caesar Salad, 33
Strawberry, Avocado, and Kale Salad, 7
Taco Salad, 3
Tropical Chicken Salad, 57

B

Bacon
  5 B Salad, 43
  Bacon and Pea Pasta Salad, 79
  Breakfast Burrito in a Jar, 103
  Broccoli, Almond, and Cherry Salad, 61
  Microwave Quiche in a Jar, 105
Bacon and Pea Pasta Salad, 79
Baguette chips
  Bruschetta and Baguette Chips, 155
Balsamic Vinaigrette, 164
  5 B Salad, 43
  Honey and Peach Panzanella, 75
  Red, White, and Blueberry Balsamic Caprese, 5
  Roasted Fall Salad, 21
Balsamic vinegar
  Balsamic Vinaigrette, 164
  Sweet Strawberry Peach Panzanella, 127
Balsamic vinegar syrup
  Sweet Strawberry Peach Panzanella, 127
Banana Cream Pie Yogurt Parfait, 90
Banana peppers
  BBQ Chicken Salad, 23
Bananas
  Banana Cream Pie Yogurt Parfait, 90
  Banana Split Trifle, 125
  Chocolate Banana Oatmeal, 98
  Peanut Butter Banana Yogurt Parfait, 90

Strawberry Banana Oatmeal, 98
Take Me Somewhere Tropical Smoothie, 94
Too Good To Be Green Smoothie, 94
Banana Split Trifle, 125
Barbecue sauce
    BBQ in a Jar, 113
    Creamy BBQ Ranch Dressing, 166
Basic Oatmeal, 98
Basic Refrigerator Oats, 86
Basic Smoothie, 94
Basic Yogurt Parfait, 90
Basil
    Asian Pear and Cashew Salad, 25
    Bruschetta and Baguette Chips, 155
    Honey and Peach Panzanella, 75
    Peach Caprese, 13
    Red, White, and Blueberry Balsamic Caprese, 5
    Sweet Strawberry Peach Panzanella, 127
BBQ Chicken Salad, 23
BBQ in a Jar, 113
Beans
    baked
        BBQ in a Jar, 113
    black
        BBQ Chicken Salad, 23
        Breakfast Burrito in a Jar, 103
        Chipotle Sweet Potato, Black Bean, and Kale Salad, 45
    cannellini
        Avocado and White Bean Salad, 73
    edamame
        Chinese Chicken Salad, 37
        Instant Noodles in a Jar, 119
        Zucchini Noodle Salad, 63
    kidney
        Rainbow Salad, 53
    refried
        Layered Dip with Tortilla Chips, 161
        Taco Bar Picnic, 115
Bean sprouts
    Asian Pear and Cashew Salad, 25
    Instant Noodles in a Jar, 119
Beef stock concentrate
    Instant Noodles in a Jar, 119
Beer
    Michelada, 145

Bell pepper. *See also* Roasted red peppers
    Asian Pear and Cashew Salad, 25
    Rainbow Salad, 53
    Thai Peanut Pasta Salad, 81
    Zucchini Noodle Salad, 63
Berry Me Smoothie, 94
Blackberries
    5 B Salad, 43
    Blackberry Crisp, 131
    Fruit Salad, 83
    Triple Berry Refrigerator Oats, 86
Blackberry Crisp, 131
Blackberry preserves
    Whiskey Jam Cocktail, 147
Blender
    handheld, xvi
    immersion, xvi
Blueberries
    Berry Me Smoothie, 94
    Fruit Salad, 83
    Peach, Blueberry, and Feta Salad, 35
    Red, White, and Blueberry Balsamic Caprese, 5
    Too Good To Be Green Smoothie, 94
    Triple Berry Refrigerator Oats, 86
Bourbon whiskey
    Whiskey Jam Cocktail, 147
Brandy
    Red Wine Camper Sangria, 139
Bread
    Chicken Parmesan "Sandwich," 107
    Honey and Peach Panzanella, 75
    Microwave Quiche in a Jar, 105
    Waldorf Chicken Salad "Sandwich," 109
Breakfast Burrito in a Jar, 103
Broccoli
    Broccoli, Almond, and Cherry Salad, 61
    Roasted Veggies, xix
Broccoli, Almond, and Cherry Salad, 61
Bruschetta and Baguette Chips, 155
Brussels sprouts
    5 B Salad, 43
    Roasted Veggies, xix
Buffalo Chicken and Quinoa Salad, 77
Buffalo sauce
    Buffalo Chicken and Quinoa Salad, 77

Butternut squash
  Roasted Fall Salad, 21
  Roasted Veggies, xix

C

Cabbage
  Rainbow Salad, 53
  Thai Peanut Pasta Salad, 81
Can coozies, xvi
Candied Nuts, xxi
  Curry Butternut Squash Salad, 39
  Honeycrisp and Spinach Salad, 47
  Peach, Blueberry, and Feta Salad, 35
Cantaloupe
  Prosciutto, Melon, and Arugula Salad, 41
Caramel
  Salted Caramel Apple Pie Trifle, 133
Carrots
  baby
    Roasted Veggies, xix
  Chinese Chicken Salad, 37
  Deconstructed Sushi, 117
  Instant Noodles in a Jar, 119
  Thai Peanut Pasta Salad, 81
Cashews
  Asian Pear and Cashew Salad, 25
Cauliflower
  Roasted Veggies, xix
Cayenne
  Candied Nuts, xxi
Celery
  Asian Pear and Cashew Salad, 25
  Buffalo Chicken and Quinoa Salad, 77
Celery salt
  Michelada, 145
Cheese
  bleu
    Buffalo Chicken and Quinoa Salad, 77
    Honeycrisp and Spinach Salad, 47
    Steak House Salad, 49
    Breakfast Burrito in a Jar, 103
  cheddar
    Bacon and Pea Pasta Salad, 79
    BBQ Chicken Salad, 23
    BBQ in a Jar, 113
    Microwave Quiche in a Jar, 105
  cotjia
    Mexican Avocado Caesar Salad, 33
    Mexican Corn Salad, 67

cream
  Garlic Lemon Feta Dip with Pretzel
  Chips, 159
  No-Bake Key Lime Cheesecake, 129
feta
  Garlic Lemon Feta Dip with Pretzel
    Chips, 159
  Mediterranean Artichoke and Spinach
    Salad, 55
  My Big Fat Greek Salad, 29
  Orzo, Spinach, and Sun-Dried Tomato
    Salad, 65
  Peach, Blueberry, and Feta Salad, 35
  Strawberry, Avocado, and Kale Salad, 7
  Zucchini Noodle Salad, 63
goat
  Mango, Strawberry, and Arugula Salad,
    27
  Pear, Pomegranate, and Spinach Salad,
    31
  Strawberry, Goat Cheese, and Spinach
    Salad, 59
  Sweet Strawberry Peach Panzanella,
    127
gorgonzola
  Arugula, Pear, and Gorgonzola Salad,
    11
Mexican
  Layered Dip with Tortilla Chips, 161
  Taco Salad, 3
mozzarella
  Antipasto Salad with Mixed Greens, 51
  Chicken Parmesan "Sandwich," 107
  Honey and Peach Panzanella, 75
  Peach Caprese, 13
  Prosciutto, Melon, and Arugula Salad,
    41
  Red, White, and Blueberry Balsamic
    Caprese, 5
Parmesan
  Chicken Parmesan "Sandwich," 107
  Cranberry and Brussels Sprouts Salad,
    15
  Creamy Polenta, 121
  Roasted Garlic Parmesan Chickpeas,
    151
  Zucchini, Corn, and Quinoa Salad, 71
Picnic in a Jar, 111

Taco Bar Picnic, 115
Cherries
    Broccoli, Almond, and Cherry Salad, 61
    Cherry Almond Oatmeal, 98
    Maraschino
        Banana Split Trifle, 125
    Pimm's Cup, 143
Cherry Almond Oatmeal, 98
Chia seeds
    Basic Refrigerator Oats, 86
Chicken
    BBQ Chicken Salad, 23
    Buffalo Chicken and Quinoa Salad, 77
    Chicken Parmesan "Sandwich," 107
    Chinese Chicken Salad, 37
    Mexican Avocado Caesar Salad, 33
    Thai Peanut Pasta Salad, 81
    Tropical Chicken Salad, 57
    Waldorf Chicken Salad "Sandwich," 109
Chicken Parmesan "Sandwich," 107
Chicken stock concentrate
    Instant Noodles in a Jar, 119
Chickpea, Avocado, and Kale Salad, 17
Chickpeas
    Chickpea, Avocado, and Kale Salad, 17
    Curry Butternut Squash Salad, 39
    My Big Fat Greek Salad, 29
    Ranch Hummus with Veggies, 153
    Roasted Garlic Parmesan Chickpeas, 151
    Sweet Potato and Chickpea Salad, 69
Chilies
    Mexican Corn Salad, 67
Chili-garlic sauce
    Instant Noodles in a Jar, 119
Chili powder
    Mexican Corn Salad, 67
Chinese Chicken Salad, 37
Chipotle Creamy Avocado Dressing, 165
    Chipotle Sweet Potato, Black Bean, and
        Kale Salad, 45
    Mexican Avocado Caesar Salad, 33
    Rainbow Salad, 53
Chipotle powder
    Chipotle Creamy Avocado Dressing,
        166
Chipotle Sweet Potato, Black Bean, and
    Kale Salad, 45
Chocolate Banana Oatmeal, 98

Chocolate chips
    Chocolate Banana Oatmeal, 98
Chocolate hazelnut spread
    Strawberry, Chocolate, and Hazelnut
        Refrigerator Oats, 86
Chocolate sauce
    Banana Split Trifle, 125
Cilantro
    Buffalo Chicken and Quinoa Salad, 77
    Chipotle Creamy Avocado Dressing, 166
    Curry Butternut Squash Salad, 39
    Guacamole Salad, 9
    Mexican Corn Salad, 67
    Spicy Cilantro Lime Vinaigrette, 164
    Strawberry Jalapeño Salsa with Cinnamon
        Sugar Pita Chips, 157
    Sweet Potato and Chickpea Salad, 69
    Thai Peanut Pasta Salad, 81
    Zucchini, Corn, and Quinoa Salad, 71
Cinnamon
    Apple Cinnamon Oatmeal, 98
    Apple Cinnamon Refrigerator Oats, 86
    Blackberry Crisp, 131
    Candied Nuts, xxi
    Pumpkin Pie Refrigerator Oats, 86
    Salted Caramel Apple Pie Trifle, 133
Cinnamon sugar pita chips
    Strawberry Jalapeño Salsa with Cinnamon
        Sugar Pita Chips, 157
Citrus Ginger Vinaigrette, 165
    Asian Pear and Cashew Salad, 25
Citrus zest
    Instant Noodles in a Jar, 119
Club soda
    Mason Jar Mojito, 141
    White Wine Camper Sangria, 137
Coconut
    Piña Colada Refrigerator Oats, 86
    Piña Colada Yogurt Parfait, 90
    Pineapple Coconut Oatmeal, 98
Coleslaw
    BBQ in a Jar, 113
Cookies
    Picnic in a Jar, 111
    Salted Caramel Apple Pie Trifle, 133
Coozies, xvi
Corn
    BBQ Chicken Salad, 23

BBQ in a Jar, 113
Buffalo Chicken and Quinoa Salad, 77
Instant Noodles in a Jar, 119
Mexican Corn Salad, 67
Steak House Salad, 49
Taco Salad, 3
Zucchini, Corn, and Quinoa Salad, 71
Cornstarch
Blackberry Crisp, 131
Crackers
Picnic in a Jar, 111
Cranberries
Cranberry and Brussels Sprouts Salad, 15
Honeycrisp and Spinach Salad, 47
Pear, Pomegranate, and Spinach Salad, 31
Waldorf Chicken Salad "Sandwich," 109
Cranberry and Brussels Sprouts Salad, 15
Creamy BBQ Ranch Dressing, 166
BBQ Chicken Salad, 23
Creamy Pesto Dressing, 167
Zucchini Noodle Salad, 63
Creamy Polenta, 121
Crema
Taco Bar Picnic, 115
Cucumber
BBQ Chicken Salad, 23
Deconstructed Sushi, 117
Green Machine Smoothie, 94
Mediterranean Artichoke and Spinach
Salad, 55
Pimm's Cup, 143
Rainbow Salad, 53
Cumin
Breakfast Burrito in a Jar, 103
Cupcake liners, xvi
Cuppow BNTO cups, xvi
Curry Butternut Squash Salad, 39
Curry paste
Instant Noodles in a Jar, 119
Curry powder
Curry Tahini Vinaigrette, 166
Curry Tahini Vinaigrette, 166
Curry Butternut Squash Salad, 39
Sweet Potato and Chickpea Salad,
69

D
Deconstructed Sushi, 117

Dijon mustard
Garlic Lemon Dijon Vinaigrette, 164
Honey-Lime Poppy Seed Dressing, 164
Dill
Garlic Lemon Feta Dip with Pretzel Chips,
159
Ranch Hummus with Veggies, 153

E
Edamame
Chinese Chicken Salad, 37
Instant Noodles in a Jar, 119
Zucchini Noodle Salad, 63
Eggs
Breakfast Burrito in a Jar, 103
Microwave Quiche in a Jar, 105
Egg whites
Candied Nuts, xxi

F
Flour
Blackberry Crisp, 131
Fruit Salad, 83

G
Garlic
Bruschetta and Baguette Chips, 155
Garlic Lemon Dijon Vinaigrette, 164
Garlic Lemon Feta Dip with Pretzel Chips,
159
Spicy Peanut Dressing, 166
Garlic Lemon Dijon Vinaigrette, 164
Avocado and White Bean Salad, 73
Cranberry and Brussels Sprouts Salad, 15
Garlic Lemon Feta Dip with Pretzel Chips,
159
Garlic paste
Instant Noodles in a Jar, 119
Garlic powder
Roasted Garlic Parmesan Chickpeas, 151
Waldorf Chicken Salad "Sandwich," 109
Garlic salt
Ranch Hummus with Veggies, 153
Ginger
pickled
Deconstructed Sushi, 117
Ginger beer
Pimm's Cup, 143

Ginger paste
  Citrus Ginger Vinaigrette, 165
  Instant Noodles in a Jar, 119
  Spicy Peanut Dressing, 166
Graham crackers
  Apple Cinnamon Refrigerator Oats, 86
  Key Lime Refrigerator Oats, 86
  No-Bake Key Lime Cheesecake, 129
Granola
  Banana Cream Pie Yogurt Parfait, 90
  Basic Yogurt Parfait, 90
  Peanut Butter Banana Yogurt Parfait, 90
  Piña Colada Yogurt Parfait, 90
  Raspberry Lemonade Yogurt Parfait, 90
Grapes
  Waldorf Chicken Salad "Sandwich," 109
Grape-seed oil
  Citrus Ginger Vinaigrette, 165
Green Machine Smoothie, 94
Guacamole
  Layered Dip with Tortilla Chips, 161
Guacamole Salad, 9

H
Half & half
  Creamy Polenta, 121
Ham
  Microwave Quiche in a Jar, 105
Hazelnuts
  Strawberry, Chocolate, and Hazelnut
    Refrigerator Oats, 86
History, of mason jar, xi
Honey
  Apple Cider Vinaigrette, 165
  Balsamic Vinaigrette, 164
  Basic Refrigerator Oats, 86
  Citrus Ginger Vinaigrette, 165
  Creamy BBQ Ranch Dressing, 166
  Garlic Lemon Dijon Vinaigrette, 164
  Honey and Peach Panzanella, 75
  Honey Lime Dressing, 167
  Honey-Lime Poppy Seed Dressing, 164
  White Balsamic Vinaigrette, 165
Honey and Peach Panzanella, 75
Honeycrisp and Spinach Salad, 47
Honey Lime Dressing, 167
  Fruit Salad, 83
Honey-Lime Poppy Seed Dressing, 164

Honey-Lime Poppy Seed Vinaigrette
  Strawberry, Avocado, and Kale Salad, 7
Hot sauce
  Instant Noodles in a Jar, 119
  Michelada, 145

I
Ice cream
  Salted Caramel Apple Pie Trifle, 133
Immersion blender, xvi
Instant Noodles in a Jar, 119

J
Jalapeño
  Spicy Cilantro Lime Vinaigrette, 164
  Strawberry Jalapeño Salsa with Cinnamon
    Sugar Pita Chips, 157

K
Kale
  Chickpea, Avocado, and Kale Salad, 17
  Chipotle Sweet Potato, Black Bean, and
    Kale Salad, 45
  Curry Butternut Squash Salad, 39
  Mexican Avocado Caesar Salad, 33
  Roasted Fall Salad, 21
  Strawberry, Avocado, and Kale Salad, 7
  Sweet Potato and Chickpea Salad, 69
  Too Good To Be Green Smoothie, 94
Key Lime Refrigerator Oats, 86
Key limes
  Key Lime Refrigerator Oats, 86
  No-Bake Key Lime Cheesecake, 129
Kiwi
Fruit Salad, 83

L
Layered Dip with Tortilla Chips, 161
Lemon juice
  Chipotle Creamy Avocado Dressing, 166
  Creamy BBQ Ranch Dressing, 166
  Curry Tahini Vinaigrette, 166
  Garlic Lemon Dijon Vinaigrette, 164
  Garlic Lemon Feta Dip with Pretzel Chips,
    159
  Green Machine Smoothie, 94
  Lemon Vinaigrette, 165
  Ranch Hummus with Veggies, 153

Waldorf Chicken Salad "Sandwich," 109
Lemon-lime soda
    Red Wine Camper Sangria, 139
Lemons
    Pimm's Cup, 143
    Red Wine Camper Sangria, 139
Lemon Vinaigrette, 165
    Broccoli, Almond, and Cherry Salad, 61
    Mediterranean Artichoke and Spinach
        Salad, 55
    My Big Fat Greek Salad, 29
    Orzo, Spinach, and Sun-Dried Tomato
        Salad, 65
Lemon zest
    Raspberry Lemonade Yogurt Parfait, 90
Lids, plastic, xvi
Limes
    Honey Lime Dressing, 167
    Honey-Lime Poppy Seed Dressing, 164
    Instant Noodles in a Jar, 119
    key
        Key Lime Refrigerator Oats, 86
        No-Bake Key Lime Cheesecake, 129
    Mason Jar Mojito, 141
    Michelada, 145
    Spicy Cilantro Lime Vinaigrette, 164
    Strawberry Jalapeño Salsa with Cinnamon
        Sugar Pita Chips, 157
Lime zest
    Honey Lime Dressing, 167
    Key Lime Refrigerator Oats, 86

M
Mango
    Mango, Strawberry, and Arugula Salad, 27
    Take Me Somewhere Tropical Smoothie,
        94
    Too Good To Be Green Smoothie, 94
    Tropical Chicken Salad, 57
Mango, Strawberry, and Arugula Salad, 27
Maraschino cherry
    Banana Split Trifle, 125
Mason, John, xi
Mason jar(s)
    attachments, xvi
    history of, xi
    types of, xiv
Mason Jar Mojito, 141

Mediterranean Artichoke and Spinach Salad,
    55
Mexican Avocado Caesar Salad, 33
Mexican beer
Michelada, 145
Mexican Corn Salad, 67
    Michelada, 145
Microwave Quiche in a Jar, 105
Milk
    almond
        Basic Refrigerator Oats, 86
        Berry Me Smoothie, 94
        Key Lime Refrigerator Oats, 86
        Pumpkin Pie Refrigerator Oats, 86
        Triple Berry Refrigerator Oats, 86
    Apple Cinnamon Oatmeal, 98
    Apple Cinnamon Refrigerator Oats, 86
    Basic Oatmeal, 98
    Basic Refrigerator Oats, 86
    Cherry Almond Oatmeal, 98
    Chocolate Banana Oatmeal, 98
    coconut
        Basic Refrigerator Oats, 86
        Key Lime Refrigerator Oats, 86
        Piña Colada Refrigerator Oats, 86
        Take Me Somewhere Tropical Smoothie,
            94
    condensed
        No-Bake Key Lime Cheesecake, 129
    Creamy Polenta, 121
    Microwave Quiche in a Jar, 105
    Pineapple Coconut Oatmeal, 98
    Strawberry, Chocolate, and Hazelnut
        Refrigerator Oats, 86
    Strawberry Banana Oatmeal, 98
Mint
    Honey and Peach Panzanella, 75
    Mason Jar Mojito, 141
    Watermelon, Feta, and Arugula Salad,
        19
Miso paste
    Instant Noodles in a Jar, 119
Mushrooms
    Instant Noodles in a Jar, 119
My Big Fat Greek Salad, 29

N
Napoleon, xi

No-Bake Key Lime Cheesecake, 129
Noodles
    Instant Noodles in a Jar, 119
Nori
    Deconstructed Sushi, 117
Nutmeg
    Apple Cinnamon Refrigerator Oats, 86
    Pumpkin Pie Refrigerator Oats, 86
Nuts, candied, xxi

O

Oats
    Apple Cinnamon Oatmeal, 98
    Apple Cinnamon Refrigerator Oats, 86
    Basic Oatmeal, 98
    Basic Refrigerator Oats, 86
    Blackberry Crisp, 131
    Cherry Almond Oatmeal, 98
    Chocolate Banana Oatmeal, 98
    Key Lime Refrigerator Oats, 86
    Piña Colada Refrigerator Oats, 86
    Pineapple Coconut Oatmeal, 98
    Pumpkin Pie Refrigerator Oats, 86
    Strawberry, Chocolate, and Hazelnut
        Refrigerator Oats, 86
    Strawberry Banana Oatmeal, 98
    Triple Berry Refrigerator Oats, 86
Olives
    Antipasto Salad with Mixed Greens,
        51
    My Big Fat Greek Salad, 29
    Orzo, Spinach, and Sun-Dried Tomato
        Salad, 65
    Zucchini Noodle Salad, 63
Onion powder
    Ranch Hummus with Veggies, 153
Orange juice
    Citrus Ginger Vinaigrette, 165
Oranges
    mandarin
    Chinese Chicken Salad, 37
    Red Wine Camper Sangria, 139
Oregano
    Roasted Garlic Parmesan Chickpeas,
        151

Orzo
    My Big Fat Greek Salad, 29
    Orzo, Spinach, and Sun-Dried Tomato
        Salad, 65
Orzo, Spinach, and Sun-Dried Tomato Salad,
65

P
Paprika
    Bacon and Pea Pasta Salad, 79
    Breakfast Burrito in a Jar, 103
Parsley
    Ranch Hummus with Veggies, 153
Pasta salad
    Picnic in a Jar, 111
Peach, Blueberry, and Feta Salad, 35
Peach Caprese, 13
Peaches
    Fruit Salad, 83
    Honey and Peach Panzanella, 75
    Peach, Blueberry, and Feta Salad, 35
    Sweet Strawberry Peach Panzanella, 127
    Take Me Somewhere Tropical Smoothie,
        94
    White Wine Camper Sangria, 137
Peach nectar
    White Wine Camper Sangria, 137
Peach purée
    White Wine Camper Sangria, 137
Peanut butter
    Peanut Butter Banana Yogurt Parfait, 90
    Spicy Peanut Dressing, 166
Peanut Butter Banana Yogurt Parfait, 90
Peanuts
    Thai Peanut Pasta Salad, 81
Pear, Pomegranate, and Spinach Salad, 31
Pears
    Arugula, Pear, and Gorgonzola Salad, 11
    Asian Pear and Cashew Salad, 25
    Pear, Pomegranate, and Spinach Salad, 31
Peas
    Bacon and Pea Pasta Salad, 79
    Instant Noodles in a Jar, 119
Pecans
    Candied Nuts, xxi
    Peach, Blueberry, and Feta Salad, 35
    Pear, Pomegranate, and Spinach Salad, 31

Pepitas
  Mexican Avocado Caesar Salad, 33
  Roasted Fall Salad, 21
Pesto
  Creamy Pesto Dressing, 167
Pickled ginger
  Deconstructed Sushi, 117
Picnic in a Jar, 111
Pimm's Cup, 143
Pimm's No. 1
  Pimm's Cup, 143
Piña Colada Refrigerator Oats, 86
Piña Colada Yogurt Parfait, 90
Pineapple
  Fruit Salad, 83
  Green Machine Smoothie, 94
  Piña Colada Refrigerator Oats, 86
  Piña Colada Yogurt Parfait, 90
  Pineapple Coconut Oatmeal, 98
  Take Me Somewhere Tropical Smoothie,
    94
  Tropical Chicken Salad, 57
Pineapple Coconut Oatmeal, 98
Pineapple preserves
  Banana Split Trifle, 125
Pine nuts
  Arugula, Pear, and Gorgonzola Salad, 11
  My Big Fat Greek Salad, 29
Polenta
  Creamy Polenta, 121
Pomegranate arils
  Pear, Pomegranate, and Spinach Salad, 31
Pomegranate seeds
  Roasted Fall Salad, 21
Poppy seeds
  Honey-Lime Poppy Seed Dressing, 164
Pork
  BBQ in a Jar, 113
Potato
  Roasted Veggies, xix
  sweet
    Chipotle Sweet Potato, Black Bean, and
      Kale Salad, 45
    Roasted Veggies, xix
    Sweet Potato and Chickpea Salad, 69
Pound cake
  Sweet Strawberry Peach Panzanella, 127

Pretzel chips
  Garlic Lemon Feta Dip with Pretzel Chips,
    159
Prosciutto
  Prosciutto, Melon, and Arugula Salad, 41
Prosciutto, Melon, and Arugula Salad, 41
Pumpkin
  Pumpkin Pie Refrigerator Oats, 86
  Roasted Veggies, xix
Pumpkin Pie Refrigerator Oats, 86
Pumpkin pie spice
  Pumpkin Pie Refrigerator Oats, 86
Pumpkin seeds
  Mexican Avocado Caesar Salad, 33
  Roasted Fall Salad, 21

Q
Quinoa
  Buffalo Chicken and Quinoa Salad, 77
  Zucchini, Corn, and Quinoa Salad, 71

R
Rainbow Salad, 53
Ranch dip seasoning mix
  Creamy BBQ Ranch Dressing, 166
Ranch dressing
  BBQ Chicken Salad, 23
  Creamy BBQ Ranch Dressing, 166
Ranch Hummus with Veggies, 153
Raspberries
  Berry Me Smoothie, 94
  Raspberry Lemonade Yogurt Parfait, 90
  Triple Berry Refrigerator Oats, 86
Raspberry Lemonade Yogurt Parfait, 90
Red, White, and Blueberry Balsamic
  Caprese, 5
Red pepper flakes
  Chickpea, Avocado, and Kale Salad, 17
Red wine
  Red Wine Camper Sangria, 139
Red Wine Camper Sangria, 139
Red Wine Vinaigrette, 165
  Antipasto Salad with Mixed Greens, 51
Red wine vinegar
  Red Wine Vinaigrette, 165
Refried beans
  Layered Dip with Tortilla Chips, 161

Rice
  Deconstructed Sushi, 117
Rice wine vinegar
  Citrus Ginger Vinaigrette, 165
  Instant Noodles in a Jar, 119
  Spicy Peanut Dressing, 166
Roasted Fall Salad, 21
Roasted Garlic Parmesan Chickpeas, 151
Roasted red peppers
  Antipasto Salad with Mixed Greens, 51
Roasted Veggies, xix
Rosemary
  Roasted Veggies, xix
Rum, white
  Mason Jar Mojito, 141

S
Salads ingredients, xii–xiii
Salad spinner, xvi
Salami
  Antipasto Salad with Mixed Greens, 51
  Picnic in a Jar, 111
Salsa
  Breakfast Burrito in a Jar, 103
  Layered Dip with Tortilla Chips, 161
  Taco Bar Picnic, 115
Salted Caramel Apple Pie Trifle, 133
Seaweed
  Deconstructed Sushi, 117
Sesame oil
  Instant Noodles in a Jar, 119
  Spicy Peanut Dressing, 166
Sesame seeds
  Citrus Ginger Vinaigrette, 165
Shallots
  Garlic Lemon Feta Dip with Pretzel Chips,
    159
  Red Wine Vinaigrette, 165
Simple syrup
  Mason Jar Mojito, 141
Sour cream
  Breakfast Burrito in a Jar, 103
  Buffalo Chicken and Quinoa Salad, 77
  Layered Dip with Tortilla Chips, 161
Soy sauce
  Instant Noodles in a Jar, 119
  Spicy Peanut Dressing, 166

Spaghetti
  Thai Peanut Pasta Salad, 81
Sparkling water, lime-flavored
  Whiskey Jam Cocktail, 147
Spicy Cilantro Lime Vinaigrette, 164
  Guacamole Salad, 9
  Mexican Corn Salad, 67
  Taco Salad, 164
  Tropical Chicken Salad, 57
  Zucchini, Corn, and Quinoa Salad, 71
Spicy Peanut Dressing, 166
  Thai Peanut Pasta Salad, 81
Spicy pickled vegetables
  Taco Bar Picnic, 115
Spinach
  Green Machine Smoothie, 94
  Honeycrisp and Spinach Salad, 47
  Instant Noodles in a Jar, 119
  Mediterranean Artichoke and Spinach
    Salad, 55
  Microwave Quiche in a Jar, 105
  My Big Fat Greek Salad, 29
  Orzo, Spinach, and Sun-Dried Tomato
    Salad, 65
  Pear, Pomegranate, and Spinach Salad, 31
  Strawberry, Goat Cheese, and Spinach
    Salad, 59
  Too Good To Be Green Smoothie, 94
  Tropical Chicken Salad, 57
Sprouts
  Asian Pear and Cashew Salad, 25
Squash
  butternut
    Curry Butternut Squash Salad, 39
    Roasted Fall Salad, 21
    Roasted Veggies, xix
Sriracha
  Spicy Peanut Dressing, 166
Steak
  Steak House Salad, 49
Steak House Salad, 49
Strawberries
  Banana Split Trifle, 125
  Berry Me Smoothie, 94
  Fruit Salad, 83
  Strawberry, Chocolate, and Hazelnut
    Refrigerator Oats, 86

Strawberry, Goat Cheese, and Spinach Salad, 59
Strawberry Banana Oatmeal, 98
Strawberry Jalapeño Salsa with Cinnamon Sugar Pita Chips, 157
Sweet Strawberry Peach Panzanella, 127
Take Me Somewhere Tropical Smoothie, 94
Too Good To Be Green Smoothie, 94
Strawberry, Avocado, and Kale Salad, 7
Strawberry, Chocolate, and Hazelnut Refrigerator Oats, 86
Strawberry, Goat Cheese, and Spinach Salad, 59
Strawberry Banana Oatmeal, 98
Strawberry Jalapeño Salsa with Cinnamon Sugar Pita Chips, 157
Sugar
    Blackberry Crisp, 131
    brown
        Apple Cinnamon Oatmeal, 98
        Basic Oatmeal, 98
        Blackberry Crisp, 131
        Cherry Almond Oatmeal, 98
        Chocolate Banana Oatmeal, 98
        Pineapple Coconut Oatmeal, 98
        Salted Caramel Apple Pie Trifle, 133
        Spicy Peanut Dressing, 166
        Strawberry Banana Oatmeal, 98
    Mason Jar Mojito, 141
    No-Bake Key Lime Cheesecake, 129
Sun-dried tomatoes
    Orzo, Spinach, and Sun-Dried Tomato Salad, 65
Sweet potato
    Roasted Veggies, xix
Sweet Potato and Chickpea Salad, 69
Sweet Strawberry Peach Panzanella, 127

T
Tabasco
    Michelada, 145
Taco Bar Picnic, 115
Taco Salad, 3
Tahini
    Curry Tahini Vinaigrette, 166
    Ranch Hummus with Veggies, 153

Take Me Somewhere Tropical Smoothie, 94
Tangerine
    Fruit Salad, 83
Thai Peanut Pasta Salad, 81
Thyme
    Garlic Lemon Dijon Vinaigrette, 164
    Roasted Veggies, xix
    Whiskey Jam Cocktail, 147
Tofu
    Instant Noodles in a Jar, 119
Tomatoes. See also Sun-dried tomatoes
    Avocado and White Bean Salad, 73
    BBQ Chicken Salad, 23
    Bruschetta and Baguette Chips, 155
    Buffalo Chicken and Quinoa Salad, 77
    Chicken Parmesan "Sandwich," 107
    Guacamole Salad, 9
    Honey and Peach Panzanella, 75
    Mediterranean Artichoke and Spinach Salad, 55
    Mexican Avocado Caesar Salad, 33
    Microwave Quiche in a Jar, 105
    My Big Fat Greek Salad, 29
    Peach Caprese, 13
    Rainbow Salad, 53
    Red, White, and Blueberry Balsamic Caprese, 5
    Sweet Potato and Chickpea Salad, 69
    Taco Salad, 3
    Zucchini, Corn, and Quinoa Salad, 71
    Zucchini Noodle Salad, 63
Tomato juice
    Michelada, 145
Tomato sauce
    Chicken Parmesan "Sandwich," 107
Too Good To Be Green Smoothie, 94
Tortilla
    Breakfast Burrito in a Jar, 103
    Taco Bar Picnic, 115
Tortilla chips
    Layered Dip with Tortilla Chips, 161
    Taco Salad, 3
Triple Berry Refrigerator Oats, 86
Tropical Chicken Salad, 57

V
Vanilla wafers
    Banana Cream Pie Yogurt Parfait, 90

Vegetables, roasted, xix
Vegetable stock concentrate
    Instant Noodles in a Jar, 119
Vinegar
    apple cider
        Apple Cider Vinaigrette, 165
    balsamic
        Balsamic Vinaigrette, 164
        Sweet Strawberry Peach Panzanella, 127
    red wine
        Red Wine Vinaigrette, 165
    rice wine
        Citrus Ginger Vinaigrette, 165
        Instant Noodles in a Jar, 119
        Spicy Peanut Dressing, 166
    white balsamic
        White Balsamic Vinaigrette, 165
    white wine
        Creamy Pesto Dressing, 167
        Curry Tahini Vinaigrette, 166
        Garlic Lemon Dijon Vinaigrette, 164
        White Wine Vinaigrette, 164
Vodka
    White Wine Camper Sangria, 137

W
Waldorf Chicken Salad "Sandwich," 109
Walnuts
    Candied Nuts, xxi
    Strawberry, Goat Cheese, and Spinach Salad, 59
Wasabi
    Deconstructed Sushi, 117
Watermelon, Feta, and Arugula Salad, 19
Whipped topping
    Banana Split Trifle, 125
    No-Bake Key Lime Cheesecake, 129
    Salted Caramel Apple Pie Trifle, 133
Whiskey Jam Cocktail, 147
White Balsamic Vinaigrette, 165
    Peach, Blueberry, and Feta Salad, 35
    Prosciutto, Melon, and Arugula Salad, 41
    Strawberry, Goat Cheese, and Spinach Salad, 59
White balsamic vinegar
    White Balsamic Vinaigrette, 165

White wine
    White Wine Camper Sangria, 137
White Wine Camper Sangria, 137
White Wine Vinaigrette, 164
    Chickpea, Avocado, and Kale Salad, 17
    Pear, Pomegranate, and Spinach Salad, 31
    Steak House Salad, 49
    Watermelon, Feta, and Arugula Salad, 19
White wine vinegar
    Creamy Pesto Dressing, 167
    Curry Tahini Vinaigrette, 166
    Garlic Lemon Dijon Vinaigrette, 164
    White Wine Vinaigrette, 164
Wine
    red
        Red Wine Camper Sangria, 139
    white
        White Wine Camper Sangria, 137
Worcestershire sauce
    Michelada, 145

Y
Yogurt
    Banana Cream Pie Yogurt Parfait, 90
    Banana Split Trifle, 125
    Basic Smoothie, 94
    Basic Yogurt Parfait, 90
    Greek
        Apple Cinnamon Refrigerator Oats, 86
        Bacon and Pea Pasta Salad, 79
        Basic Refrigerator Oats, 86
        Berry Me Smoothie, 94
        Broccoli, Almond, and Cherry Salad, 61
        Chicken Parmesan "Sandwich," 107
        Chipotle Creamy Avocado Dressing, 166
        Creamy BBQ Ranch Dressing, 166
        Creamy Pesto Dressing, 167
        Honey Lime Dressing, 167
        Key Lime Refrigerator Oats, 86
        Mexican Corn Salad, 67
        Piña Colada Refrigerator Oats, 86
        Pumpkin Pie Refrigerator Oats, 86
        Ranch Hummus with Veggies, 153
        Strawberry, Chocolate, and Hazelnut Refrigerator Oats, 86
        Triple Berry Refrigerator Oats, 86
        Waldorf Chicken Salad "Sandwich," 109

Peanut Butter Banana Yogurt Parfait, 90
Piña Colada Yogurt Parfait, 90
Raspberry Lemonade Yogurt Parfait, 90

Z
Zucchini
    Instant Noodles in a Jar, 119
    My Big Fat Greek Salad, 29
    Zucchini, Corn, and Quinoa Salad, 71
    Zucchini Noodle Salad, 63
Zucchini, Corn, and Quinoa Salad, 71
Zucchini Noodle Salad, 63